THE FORGOTTEN AMERICANS

THE FORGOTTEN AMERICANS

JOHN E. SCHWARZ

A N D

Thomas J. Volgy

W · W · NORTON & COMPANY

New York

London

The text of this book is composed in 11/13 Sabon
with the display set in ITC Garamond Book Condensed
Composition and manufacturing
by The Maple-Vail Book Manufacturing Group.
Book design by Margaret M. Wagner.

Library of Congress Cataloging in Publication Data
Schwarz, John E.
    The forgotten Americans / John E. Schwarz and Thomas J. Volgy.
p.   cm.
1. Poor—United States.   2. Working class—United States.
I. Volgy, Thomas J.   II. Title.
HC110.P6S32   1992
395.305.5′69′0973—dc20   91–39019

ISBN 0-393-03388-0

W. W. Norton & Company, Inc.
500 Fifth Avenue, New York, N.Y. 10110
W. W. Norton & Company Ltd.
10 Coptic Street, London WC1A 1PU

    2 3 4 5 6 7 8 9 0

To the families whose lives are described in this book and whose courage and dignity are a continual inspiration.

It is but equity . . . *that they who feed, cloath and lodge the whole body of the people, should have such a share of the produce of their own labour as to be themselves tolerably well fed, cloathed and lodged.*

Adam Smith
The Wealth of Nations

The dream from which we must be woken is the dream that all is well. The most dangerous illusion of them all is the illusion that all is well.

William Nicholson
Shadowlands

CONTENTS

Contents

LIST OF TABLES

PREFACE

"The forgotten man at the bottom of the economic pyramid" were the words Franklin Roosevelt used in early 1932, nearly a year prior to his election. Hardworking Americans who live in need were forgotten then and are largely forgotten today. Some observers presume that the condition of working poverty does not exist in this country for wage earners who are diligent and stay on the job; others vastly underestimate its scale. To do otherwise requires having to face the reality, with its many implications, that America may not be the land of opportunity it claims to be, not even for people who are diligent, responsible workers. *The Forgotten Americans* is written about these people, numbering in the tens of millions including their families, whom the nation has forgotten and the government's policies have failed, to the detriment of us all.

The research and the writing of the book benefited from the help and advice of many people. Every page of it owes much to them. Among those on the faculty of the University of Arizona, and other universities, who made important contributions are James Clarke, John Crow, Vine Deloria, Paula England, Susan Gonzalez-Baker, Richard Jankowski, Ron Replogle, Lawrence Scaff, James Shockey, and Deborah Stone. Thanks are also due to a highly talented group of staff and graduate students at the University of Arizona: Bill Lockwood, Jan Thompson, Kelli Waldron, Steven Brundage, Randy Carnahan, Sherry Dillard, Jennifer Dubois, Hungder Fu, Ismalizah Ismail, Becky Killion, John Smith, and Gwen Torges. Many personal friends, too, like Barbara Kingsolver, David Lasker, Ann Nichols, and Cindy Resnick, were always there when needed. A close friend, Jacqueline Sharkey, helped mold and shape the book with her valuable insights on nearly a weekly basis over a three-year period. The ideas of Judi, Jodi, Jennifer, and Laurie Schwarz are also found in numerous places in the book. Thanks also go to Susan Dubow. In addition, a special debt is owed the families whose profiles appear in the book and to whom the book is dedicated. If the book helps address their plight, which many others share, that debt will be only partly repaid. Finally, the efforts of Roby Harrington, Henning Gutmann, Nancy Yanchus, Jean Yelovich, and others at W. W. Norton were beyond compare. Any success the book achieves will have been made possible by them.

Responsibility for the errors that remain, of course, lies with us. John E. Schwarz is the principal author of chapters 1 through 6, chapter 8, and the appendix. Thomas J. Volgy is the principal author of chapter 7. The two of us combined to write the epilogue.

THE FORGOTTEN AMERICANS

THE AMERICAN ETHOS
AND THE AMERICAN
PEOPLE

Americans have always believed that in a free society people showing individual responsibility and diligence will get ahead. So deeply ingrained is this belief that it is known as the American ethos. Yet each day millions of responsible Americans return home from their jobs to lives of enduring economic struggle. All of them are employed full-time the entire year and conscientiously practice the work ethic. Despite their hard work, they live in poverty. They and their families cannot afford the basic necessities of food, housing, clothing, and medical care, not even at the lowest realistic cost. Moreover, the limited opportunities that are available confine still other workers to more-marginal employment. Forced to piece together part-year and part-time jobs, they often fashion the hours of more than one job into what amounts to full-time work. Nonetheless, these workers, too, remain poor.

The actual number of Americans experiencing working poverty is more than double the official estimates. Including family members, nearly thirty million people—the equivalent of every man, woman, and child residing in the nation's twenty-five largest cities—live in this condition, and this figure describes the situation in America during *favorable* economic times. During recession, the tragedy worsens.

The many working Americans who are left in poverty, even in times of prosperity, dispel conventional wisdom in another way, too. They come from an extraordinarily wide variety of backgrounds. Individuals who have historically encountered discrimination in this country are among them, yet so are countless others coming from sectors of the society often thought to have advantages.

In the past, the nation's great political struggles often focused on extending the fruits of freedom and economic opportunity to every American. During the early years of our country, the American ethos was restricted to free white males. The Civil War brought black Americans out of slavery. The suffrage movement of the early decades of the twentieth century secured the vote for women. The civil rights movement of the 1950s, 1960s, and 1970s addressed the issue of equal opportunity for Americans regardless of race or gender. Over time, the American ethos and the philosophy of freedom and opportunity have gradually expanded to embrace ever more groups. Despite this, racial minorities and women still suffer disproportionately. Dramatic discrepancies exist between the rewards that they are supposed to obtain from employment and the harsh realities they encounter as they try to provide food, shelter, and clothing for their families.

However, this is only a small part of the problem. Families of all kinds are left clawing at the edges of the economy despite their painstaking efforts and the fact that they are employed in wide-ranging occupations across nearly all the industrial and business sectors. The failure of hard work in this country to result in a minimally decent return transcends the boundaries of race or gender, and even of workers' educational credentials. People who are male and white make up the largest group of employed heads of household who live in poverty. Rather than being school dropouts, the great majority of workers who remain poor have completed a high school education or gone to college. Many, indeed, rank in the upper half of the nation in academic skills.

During the past several years, newspapers and television newscasts have featured dozens of stories about a group called the new poor. The term "new poor" refers to middle-class citizens who lost their jobs—a large number of them during the recession of the early 1990s—and joined the ranks of the poor. Many of them remain without work. Once contributors to charity, the new poor find that they themselves may now in desperation have to turn to charity for food, clothing, and housing. Some stand in food lines. Their descent has been a brutal one.

The attention given to the new poor has awakened the public's consciousness to the fact that Americans who have followed all the rules may be unable to provide adequately for their families. This may appear to be new in America; however, it is not new at all. Millions of Americans, even though employed full-time, had insufficient incomes to afford food, clothing, and housing prior to the recession, during the prosperous years of the 1980s, and long before that too.[1] These are the forgotten Americans. A crucial difference distinguishes the two groups. The new poor are hardworking people who became poor upon losing their jobs; the forgotten Americans are hardworking people who remain poor despite holding jobs. It is to be hoped that most of the new poor will regain their former economic status with the economy's recovery. Yet it is likely that some of them will not and ultimately may become members of the working poor. Some already have joined the ranks of the forgotten Americans, forced into jobs at low wages with few or no benefits.

The Forgotten Americans describes the lives of industrious people who receive so little in return for hard work that they are unable to escape poverty. Their bitter experience violates the most fundamental precepts of the nation, expressed in the American ethos. At the same time, it contravenes basic norms of equity, as the philosopher Adam Smith observed long ago. Simple equity, he held, dictates that it is wrong that workers who feed, clothe, and house the nation do not themselves enjoy a tolerable standard of living.[2] The widespread presence of working poverty, in turn, undermines the ability of the nation to address a series of other issues of concern to Americans. Low pay devalues rather than rewards the work ethic. When many people find that a paycheck and poverty come in the same envelope, welfare dependency and other conditions related to poverty, such as crime and drug dealing, become aggravated and their alleviation far more difficult. Until working poverty is clearly understood and properly addressed, the current debate over welfare reform cannot be successfully resolved.

The recession of the early 1990s and cutbacks in both employment and pay led many Americans to ask whether the grim fate of the working poor might not someday be their own. It was not solely the new poor but also middle-class workers still holding decent jobs who began to wonder whether and when their time might come. The surprising breadth and extent of working poverty that exists in America, which this book discloses, permits a sure prediction. Unless corrective action is taken, poverty will pervade the lives of no fewer than tens of millions of American workers and their families indefinitely into the future. The new poor and others who enter the ranks of the working poor will simply add to these numbers. Corrective action can successfully attack the condition of working poverty, but only if it builds upon fresh thinking. Working poverty casts a very wide net. Because it is so deeply entrenched in America, even when the economy is strong, the remedy for resolving it and providing all Americans with greater security will require prescriptions reaching beyond the policy answers that currently hold sway in the nation and the theories of poverty that have been used to justify them. In spite of the adversity that millions of workers have suffered for many years, the American ethos has nevertheless retained considerable force in the nation's consciousness. Since the country's inception, the ethos of individual advancement and success has been basic to the way Americans have thought about the nation and about themselves. It largely continues that way today, and for good reason. Unlike many peoples, Americans do not have a common blood, religion, race, or language. Absent the bonds that often link individuals in a nation, Americans have forged a national identity and sense of connection to one another out of other materials. They have done so, to a considerable extent, through a shared philosophy founded upon a belief in the promise, possibilities, and progress of the individual. It is captured in numerous commonplace sayings: "Hard work pays off"; "Keep at it and you'll succeed"; "You can't keep a good person down." The faith that responsible, hardworking individuals will rise in America expresses the spirit of this country. This ethos is felt so viscerally, that the historian Louis Hartz called it America's nationalism.[3]

The ethos depicts a fundamental way in which all Americans share a birthright in this nation of otherwise kaleidoscopic differences. At its core, the ethos is a belief in inclusion. It is a belief that all can belong no matter what their background or station, that everyone can succeed. The ethos has never claimed that everyone who works hard will gain equal economic success. By virtue of exceptional ambition, special talent, or plain luck, some hardworking Americans will become fabulously wealthy, whereas others will not. The ethos assumes that economic differences among Americans will and, indeed, should occur. But it is expected that educational and occupational opportunities will be plentiful enough that all Americans, if they are diligent, can share at least a part of the good life. Everyone can find a respectable place. All who are conscientious can, at a minimum, make their way.

At the birth of the Republic, Benjamin Franklin described how it was supposed to work: "If they are poor [in America], they first begin as Servants or Journeymen; and if they are sober, industrious, and frugal, they soon become Masters, establish themselves in Business, marry, raise Families, and become respectable Citizens."[4] Many of Franklin's contemporaries held a similar view.[5] Two centuries later, the sociologist Robert Bellah, recounting the belief that Franklin and others had in the capacity of hardworking and responsible individuals to improve their lives in America, wrote that this potential is "what many felt in the eighteenth century—and many have felt ever since—to be the most important thing about America."[6]

The ethos came to full bloom during the latter half of the nineteenth century, celebrated through the stories of Horatio Alger. Alger, the son of a Unitarian minister, graduated from Harvard College and then became a minister himself; he left the ministry in 1866, at the age of thirty-five, to preach the gospel of success. In 1867, his first story for juveniles appeared in print. Titled *Ragged Dick* (probably a play on Franklin's "Poor Richard"),[7] the book showed through its main character how, in America, people who are poor can rise to respectability through hard work, honesty, bravery, and ambition. This and dozens of other juvenile stories made Alger the nation's foremost popularizer of the American ideal of the self-made individual.

Each of the main characters in Alger's dozens of stories achieves success. In *Ragged Dick,* the wealthy benefactor, Mr. Whitney, nicely capsulizes the American ethos when he tells the bootblack, Dick, "I hope, my lad, you will prosper and rise in the world. You know in this free country poverty in early life is no bar to a man's advancement. . . . Remember that your future position depends mainly on yourself and that it will be as high or low as you choose to make it."[8]

Alger grounded his beliefs about the progress of free individuals on the Calvinistic tenet that God rewarded the virtuous, the same idea that had originally drawn him to the ministry. His depictions of the ascent of poverty-stricken individuals found a receptive audience among nineteenth- and early-twentieth-century Americans who fully embraced the philosophy of self-help and rugged individualism. So, too, did the ideas of Adam Smith, whose economic theory from a century earlier expressed a similar optimism about the ultimate success that would come to the hardworking person, thanks to the operation of the free market.[9] At the time Alger wrote his rags-to-riches stories and Adam Smith's philosophy took root, manuals advising readers about how to achieve success could be found everywhere in America, with titles that would look familiar on today's bookshelves: *The Art of Money Making* (1872), *The Secret of Success in Life* (1881), *How to Succeed* (1882), *The Keys to Success* (1898), and *The Attainment of Success* (1907).[10]

If we accept the American ethos as an expression of reality, a crucial implication is that the existence of poverty must result largely from the personal inadequacies of the poor, a view that has been popular in America since the beginning. During the early years of the Republic, the Philadelphian Matthew Carey observed, "Many citizens entertain an idea . . . that if not the whole, at least the chief part of the distresses of the poor, arises from idleness, dissipation, and worthlessness."[11] Later, during the era of Alger, the essayist William Graham Sumner described the poor in America as "the shiftless, the imprudent, the negligent, the impractical, and the inefficient."[12] Americans have indeed been inclined to regard able-bodied men and women of working age who end up in poverty and dependent upon public assistance as something like second-class citizens, unworthy of the full respect of the community.[13]

Only in the early 1930s, in the midst of the Great Depression, did this view dramatically change, a shift that was to last for nearly forty years. With no end of the depression in sight, the federal government embraced the idea that responsible hardworking people are sometimes unable to make their way. In a sudden burst of energy, it enacted sweeping programs that created jobs, established a minimum wage, and provided relief to those without jobs.

This New Deal outlook guided policy through much of the 1960s, providing the undergirding for the War on Poverty. Stumping for his program to eliminate poverty from America, President Lyndon Johnson said, "Do something we can be proud of. Help the [poor] and lift them up and help them train and give them an education where they can make their own way. . . . We have a right to expect a job to provide food for our family, a roof over [our] head, clothes for [our] body, and with your help and with God's help we will have it in America." The War on Poverty sought to provide opportunities that would enable poor Americans, who faced circumstances beyond their control, to become self-sufficient.[14] "A hand up, not a handout" was the idea.

Public favor faded, however, when increased spending on programs for the poor after 1965 resulted in only a brief spurt of success in reducing the rate of poverty. Those years created many millions of new jobs—twenty-eight million in all from 1965 to 1980. Yet, despite the Great Society programs and the stunning growth in jobs, the percentage of people who were officially poor did not change substantially during the decade of the 1970s, and the number of people unemployed and on the welfare rolls actually rose.[15] Whether or not its conclusions were fair,[16] the public began to believe that assistance programs themselves contributed to the rising unemployment and dependency by reducing the incentives to work. Nearly two-thirds of all Americans held this opinion.[17] "Our current welfare program," Ronald Reagan said in 1988, "originally designed to raise people out of poverty, has become a crippling poverty trap, destroying families and condemning generations to dependency."[18] The political scientist Lawrence Mead summarized the issue the way many Americans understood it when he wrote that, in today's economy, few adults who work steadily full-time will remain poor.[19] It was believed that opportunity was available for nearly all and that anyone could make it who stayed on the job rather than abstaining from work and falling prey to the temptations of welfare.[20]

In this manner, the public had come full circle, once again seeing poverty not as a problem that afflicted hardworking and diligent people but as one that befell the idle and the irresolute. In 1980, for example, unemployment stood at a recessionary 7.5 percent, with more than eight million Americans out of jobs. Surveys during that year nevertheless indicated that about 70 percent of the public thought that the economic opportunities available to the poor were either "very good" or "good."[21] Two-thirds believed that opportunities for the poor were the same as or better than those for the average American.[22] Why, then, did some Americans remain poor? In the public's mind, the foremost causes of poverty were that the poor weren't thrifty, that they did not put in the needed effort, and that they lacked ability or talent.[23] Popular majorities did not consider any other factor to be a very important cause of poverty—not low wages, or a scarcity of jobs, or discrimination, or even sickness. Opinion did not change much as the 1980s advanced, either. In surveys taken in 1984 and in 1989, the Gallup organization found that 64 percent and 55 percent of the public, respectively, believed that lack of effort by the poor was the principal reason for poverty, or a reason at least equal to any that was beyond a person's control.[24]

This climate of opinion, in turn, led political leaders at all levels, and in both political parties, to call for reform in the nation's social policy, and particularly its welfare system.[25] The main problem, as they saw it, was how to get nonworking people to seek and take jobs in order to become self-sufficient rather than to continue to languish on welfare. The Reagan administration's repeated attempts to persuade Congress to reduce welfare spending and to restrict eligibility for welfare programs rested on the reasoning that these programs caused dependency. Welfare stifled people's motivation to work and thereby to become self-supporting, Reagan claimed. Republican leaders proposed reforms that would require recipients to work or at least to train for work.[26] Democrats joined Republicans to endorse the idea that individuals could rise out of poverty, and become self-supporting, through employment.[27] Democrats differed only in their contention that reaching this goal would require employment incentives. These would take the form, for example, of day-care allowances, health insurance, and the enforcement of child assistance payments from absent parents. Since the jobs for which many welfare recipients would be initially eligible often provided no health care or child care benefits, Democrats argued incentives were needed; otherwise many of the recipients would become worse off financially if they accepted the jobs than if they stayed on welfare.

Party leaders eventually compromised in 1988 and enacted major welfare reform legislation, whose implementation was to begin by the end of 1990 and to become fully operational by 1994. The reform established the Job Opportunities and Basic Skills Training Program (JOBS), often known as workfare. Workfare provided that able-bodied recipients of welfare, except those with small children, would eventually remain eligible for assistance only if they met certain work requirements. Recipients would have to participate in training programs or other activities designed to prepare them for employment, or gain actual work experience through community programs. Once they had gotten jobs, public assistance would continue to give child care and health insurance benefits for a year to those whose jobs did not provide such benefits. Proponents of reform believed that by requiring nonworking people to act responsibly, and by increasing the economic incentives for them to do so, workfare would move welfare recipients into employment enabling them to become sufficiently self-supporting so as eventually to be weaned off welfare.

In truth, workfare reformers asked no more, or less, from social policy than did the earlier architects of the Great Society and the New Deal. In America, social policy has always had the objective of lifting the poor to independence. Policymakers have always thought that public assistance should aid the able-bodied of working age only temporarily, until employment becomes available and enables them to care for themselves.[28] Unlike America, most other Western nations presume that adult citizens will remain recipients of public aid throughout much of their lives, whether they are employed or unemployed. Among the multiplicity of provisions available to all families in those countries, regardless of employment status, is access to medical care from a national health system as well as payments to assist every family with children in the form of regular (usually monthly) stipends. With the exception of assistance to the elderly, American social programs tend to be more limited in scope and to leave people at lower income levels more on their own than is the case in other democracies (see table 1).

Americans, apt to believe that with enough freedom and opportunity hardworking individuals can provide for themselves, see little reason to call for sweeping governmental intervention to aid the poor. The problem is that this belief does not reflect reality. The lives of workers from nearly every kind of background across America belie the ethos. Whether the economy is experiencing substantial growth or not, millions of fully employed Americans cannot meet their families' basic needs, and millions more work hard, sometimes in more than one job, because they are unable to find year-round full-time employment. In fact, about 40 percent of all year-round full-time workers in this nation cannot have

Table 1

THE RELATIVE SIZE AND IMPACT OF SOCIAL PROGRAMS
IN SEVEN WESTERN NATIONS

	Percentage of All Low-Income Persons Whom Governmental Benefits Lift to Half the Median Income	Percentage of All Low-Income, Two-Parent Families That Governmental Benefits Lift to Half the Median Income	Percentage of All Elderly Low-Income Families That Governmental Benefits Lift to Half the Median Income
United States	38.1	19.4	71.5
Israel	50.0	42.9	58.1
Canada	52.7	40.5	84.4
Norway	80.1	56.4	94.0
West Germany	78.8	69.8	88.4
United Kingdom	68.5	63.1	77.0
Sweden	87.8	76.5	99.9

Adapted from Timothy M. Smeeding et al., eds., *Poverty, Inequality, and Income Distribution in Comparative Perspective* (New York: Harvester, 1990), table 2.1, pp. 30–31, and table 3.5, p. 67.

the kind of family sometimes described as the American ideal—two parents and two children with one parent gainfully employed and the other at home—and simultaneously escape poverty. The American production worker earns wages so low that the average hourly pay lifts a family of four barely to the margins of poverty even if the worker is employed full-time the whole year. The nation's guiding beliefs and public policies are based on false assumptions about the relationship between poverty and work.

In the past, whenever reality contradicted the American ethos, people could say that the country was young and expanding its frontiers, that the nation had only begun to tap its vast natural resources,[29] and that the future held the potential of nearly unlimited progress. Now that no new frontiers are left to be explored and settled, however, unquestioning faith in a future of boundless opportunity and adequate provision for all those who work hard seems less tenable. To leave large numbers of hardworking and responsible people in or near poverty, without the promise of a decent and secure living standard in the future, threatens to create a deeply fractured society based on profound class divisions. The pages to come are about Americans who occupy the frontlines of the economic struggle today and about the implications of their plight for the nation's present policies and for the theories of economic hardship from which the policies derive. The book concludes by offering solutions necessary to improve the lives of these Americans and assure that millions of others will never share their fate.

C h a p t e r   T w o

ON THE ECONOMIC FRONT LINES: TWO AMERICAN FAMILIES*

We can talk about poverty, the millions of working poor, and the viability of the welfare system, but only by understanding how these abstract notions play out in the lives of hardworking Americans can we cut through the numbing statistics and conflicting arguments. Paul and Jane Lambert and Ernst and Anna Bartelle have always been hardworking and ambitious people. Yet their best efforts have fallen short. Each of the families has experienced happiness, but each has known far more pain and bitterness, outgrowths of the economic struggles that have permeated their lives and left them feeling helpless. By speaking with them, I came to understand better the complexity of the problem and the sheer despair felt by people who work hard but cannot provide adequately for their own families.

---

* The interviews of families here and elsewhere in the book were conducted and tape-recorded by John E. Schwarz. The names of persons and places of residence and employment have been changed.

PAUL AND JANE LAMBERT

Paul Lambert and his family's problems did not start the day he lost his job at Andrews' Electronics. At the time I interviewed Paul and his wife, Jane, in the summer of 1990, he was working forty-five hours a week at two part-time jobs, one taking phone orders at Sears and the other as a sales clerk at a local department store. He had been laid off from Andrews' Electronics five months earlier, at the age of thirty-nine. The two part-time jobs were the best he could find, he said. We were in their mobile home set amid two dozen others in a rural section on the outskirts of Cleveland, Ohio. Before the layoff, Paul had been the supervisor of the shipping and receiving department at Andrews', where he had worked for a year. He told me that he'd been let go when the parent company of the firm went into bankruptcy. As he spoke, he suddenly seemed ill at ease, almost as if he thought that I might not believe him. Jane, thirty-seven, worked full-time in a salaried position. She was the office manager of a warehouse, where she was responsible for answering the phones, typing, filing, and reception.

The three of us sat at a Formica table in the Lamberts' kitchen. It looked out into a spacious, though sparsely furnished, living room. A large, overstuffed armchair with a guitar resting beside it stood at the far end of the room. One of the Lamberts' three children, Ann, ten, lay comfortably on the chair with her legs dangling over the side, reading a book. The Lamberts' other two children—Ken, sixteen, and Marcy, six—were chattering playfully in another corner of the room.

The experience of being laid off and unable to find another full-time job had not taken the luster out of Paul's brown eyes. He had a gently rounded face and a kind smile, its warmth marred slightly by a badly capped tooth set against another that had broken in half. He looked directly at me as we talked, save only for brief moments when his eyes drifted away, giving him pause to gather his thoughts.

Paul had gotten one part-time job within two weeks of his layoff and the other several weeks later. He had not taken unemployment while he looked for a permanent job, and I wondered why. Paul's answers were usually to the point, and it was obvious that he had given much consideration to this one. "I could be getting $123 a week on unemployment right now," he said. He wasn't clearing a lot more than that a week ($155, at about $4.25 an hour) from the forty-five hours he worked on his two part-time jobs. "But I want to work, and unemployment is degrading," he continued. A good musician, Paul also earned a little money playing guitar at a nearby restaurant several evenings a month.

He had been searching now for five months for a permanent full-time job through the state job-placement service, two private employment agencies, and ads in the local newspaper. "I've sent more than one hundred letters out and gotten only two responses," he said. "The agencies have done nothing. It's frustrating."

Apart from his layoff from Andrews' Electronics, Paul had always had a regular full-time job. So had Jane since 1984, when she became employed as a warehouse office manager. Although both of them held full-time jobs, things had never been easy—in fact, not really much easier than when I spoke with them. From 1982 until he took the job at Andrews' Electronics, Paul was employed at Doby's, a chain drugstore with a large liquor department. He started there as assistant manager of the liquor department. Three years later, in 1985, he became manager of the department. Four of the store's employees worked under him. In 1988, his last full year at Doby's, Paul made $5.50 an hour as the liquor department manager and was on the job about forty-four hours a week. Jane, who was on salary, made $10,000 for the year, about $5 an hour. Their combined income was $22,300 that year.

Paul's face tensed as he talked about his seven years at Doby's. During all that time, he and Jane never had enough money to catch up with their bills, he said. Their three-bedroom mobile home, simple but spacious enough for a family of five, cost $470 a month in addition to $150 for utilities and phone. Their food bill was between $90 and $100 a week; they kept it to that level by clipping coupons and looking for bargains and specials. "Someday, I wish I could go to the grocery store without coupons," Jane said. They had two ancient cars, a 1974 Oldsmobile and a 1965 Ford with a sign reading "Dad's Limo" in the rear window. Each car had gone more than 300,000 miles. Since the closest public transportation was more than a mile away and unreliable, both Paul and Jane drove to work. Car insurance, gas, repairs, and license fees had cost them nearly $3,000 in 1988. Doby's provided medical insurance for the family, but the employee premiums were $800 a year, and doctors' bills and prescriptions that were not covered came to another $600. They had no dental insurance. They spent only $400 on clothes in 1988, and almost all of that went for children's clothing purchased in resale stores. Except for underwear and socks, Paul and Jane have bought no clothes for themselves, new or used, for a number of years. "I take care of my shoes so well that they come back into style," Paul joked. The last shoes he could remember buying were a pair of sneakers that cost $8.99. He couldn't remember when he had bought them. Taxes were another major expense. Federal income, Social Security, and state income taxes came to about $2,800 in 1988. These expenses totaled nearly $20,000. This left about $2,000 to cover everything else, including the purchase of school supplies for the children, replacing an old mattress, fixing a broken washing machine, repairing a vacuum cleaner, getting a daily newspaper, buying postage to pay the bills, and purchasing nonfood items like sheets and towels, paper products, cleaning supplies, shaving cream, shampoo, soap, toothbrushes, toothpaste, and light bulbs.

"We were always struggling, always behind when I was at Doby's. We never were able to make it," Paul said. "I was managing a department and getting nowhere."

They went without many things. They hadn't gone out to eat "within living memory, not to a McDonald's or anywhere else," Paul said when talking about his and his family's situation not just since his layoff but over the preceding decade. They hadn't gone to any movies, either. Nor had they taken their children out on day trips during weekends, although they had wanted to, because they felt they couldn't afford the gas. Since they had no dental insurance, Paul and Jane hadn't seen a dentist in years. Their two daughters had *never* been to a dentist, and their son had gone only because his grandma paid, Jane said. I asked Jane when she had last bought a nice dress. "When I got married," she answered. "Do you ever run out of money for food?" I inquired. "Not really, because I've always had my parents," Jane said. "If I run a bit desperate, they lend me money."

To keep going, Jane and Paul have frequently had to rely on help from others. Their landlord has fixed their cars at cost and often has lent them some of the money for parts. Paul said, " 'Whenever you can come up with any money, whenever you have a little extra,' my landlord says, 'you can pay me back.' " The last time his landlord fixed the Oldsmobile, it cost more than $400, but Paul could pay only $250, some of which he had gotten from Jane's parents. He has not yet been able to pay the rest of the bill. Relatives have also paid for the Lamberts' only vacations. Paul's brother gave him the money to go to Minnesota for a few days in 1987 to visit his aged father, who lives in a rest home there. He paid for Paul and Jane to take a similar trip in 1989. Jane's grandmother paid for Ken, the Lamberts' son, to visit her in Atlanta. Jane's parents, who run a bakery shop, sometimes have helped pay the rent. They also have bought new school clothes for the girls and helped with the car repairs. A year ago, Ken wanted a pair of Air Jordan athletic shoes, which were the rage at the time. They cost $100, a price the Lamberts couldn't begin to afford. "When Ken went to Atlanta, his grandmother bought them," Paul said with anguish, still upset about the episode.

Accepting help from others was not easy for Paul. He was appreciative. Yet he felt that he appeared deficient in the eyes of the people whose help he received, people with whom he associated every day. Moreover, he never knew whether he would get help or for what. It was unpredictable. And, even with the help, Jane and he remained unable to do many seemingly basic things in life, such as to take their family on an outing or to go to a movie, to get clothes for themselves, or to go to the dentist.

The daily battle to pay for essentials and provide for the family was not the only problem with his managerial job at Doby's. "The job was full of stress," Paul said. By his final year there, several of the workers in the main part of the store had quit. He mentioned that things weren't much better in the liquor department. "The district management was in constant flux. For example, they didn't fill my stock orders properly, which angered my customers when they couldn't find what they wanted. Sometimes customers would get physical. Some of them might have already had a drink or two, or might have been on drugs. One time a customer, angry that his favorite wasn't there, came up to me, pushed his body right up to mine, and pointed his finger right into my face. Between that kind of thing and the tension with the management, it was an everyday squeeze. One day, one of the workers in the general retail section collapsed and just dropped dead, right there, right there at the store. Died of a heart attack."

"When Jim died," Paul continued, "I knew it had to be done. I knew I had to find something else. A doctor had been telling me to quit for some time, saying I was going to have a heart attack if I didn't. He said, 'Either get out or die.' My blood pressure was sky-high. And I wasn't making enough money. At home, I was no fun to be with. I wouldn't talk for days when I got home. I didn't want to be bothered by anybody. Basically, I was just a paycheck, and the paycheck wasn't much. Jane had to raise the family by herself, no different than a single parent." After Jim died, Paul began looking for another job. When he found one at Andrews' Electronics, he left Doby's.

As Jane recalled those years, her eyes filled with tears. "I didn't know what was happening, because Paul wouldn't talk. He sat in a corner by himself." She paused, her whole face tight. She took a deep breath but was unable to continue.

Paul started at Andrews' Electronics as an assembler at $4.50 an hour. Within half a year, he had become the supervisor of the shipping and receiving department at double his original wage. They had begun to catch up with their rent, had completely paid off a doctor's bill from an illness of one of the children, and were thinking about the possibility of a family vacation. A mere half year later, he was laid off. Paul showed me a letter written by the general manager of Andrews' Electronics requesting a midyear wage raise for him. It was written about three months before the parent company went into bankruptcy:

> The intent of this letter is to give recognition to Paul Lambert for his exceptional performance in the shipping and receiving department. Paul has been and will continue to be an asset to this company. Since Paul has arrived, his subsequent performance has resolved many recurring problems and inadequacies. Paul has been highly productive on the most demanding shipping and receiving workloads. He has been instrumental in initiating new tracking procedures for parts shipped out which has made record checks much simpler and less time consuming.
>
> Paul was able to climb the ladder of command in a very short period of time to take full responsibility of purchasing, material control, and shipping and receiving. He has been a most conscientious employee and has made my responsibility

much easier with his "can do" attitude. I believe Paul should be given appropriate consideration for his abilities and effort. Thank you.

Since his layoff from Andrews' Electronics, Paul and Jane have lived on an income of about $19,000 a year. Together, they work eighty-five hours a week, and Paul continues to search for another job. They face the same financial problems they had during the seven years Paul worked at Doby's. They are behind on their rent and will turn once more to her parents. One of their cars is broken. They have no money to get it fixed. Meanwhile, school starts on Monday, and Paul and Jane have no money to buy the children the clothes they need.

I wondered whether Paul and Jane had considered getting additional education. Both had completed high school, but neither of them had attended college. "I want my kids to go to college," Paul answered. "That's the only way for them to make it these days. But when I was a kid in school, we were taught that a high school diploma is good enough. So I went into the Army, soon as I finished school. Now I've got a lot of experience. I've got ten years in management positions. That's as good as college. All the jobs say, 'Either college or experience.' The only jobs that've answered my applications have said, 'You've got too much management experience. You're overqualified.' " Paul's father, who owned a small restaurant in Minneapolis, had also finished his high school education and decided not to attend college. So had his two brothers. His mother, who was a certified public accountant, had received a college degree.

Paul looked straight at me: "You know," he said, "I was talking to a friend of mine the other day. We want to make a decent living. We've been eating it. For a long time—for many years—we've been on the other end of the stick. We've been beat into a corner. How do you get to where we can do what we need to do to survive? I've got other friends like this. They're crazed because they can't make it. I don't care if I leave." Stunned at the sudden turn of the conversation, I said, "You mean 'die'?" He reflected a moment, his eyes looking toward the floor. "Yes," he said.

ERNST AND ANNA BARTELLE

Ernst Bartelle stood with a slight stoop on the ball field, surrounded by several teenage boys. He squinted in the sun that glanced off his tanned face. He was short, no more than five foot six, and the boys towered over him. He looked to be in his fifties, with a slight paunch, wispy gray hair, and a small bald spot at the crown of his head. His skin had begun to sag under the chin. His face was angular, with high cheekbones and a broad, almost bulbous nose. The boys were laughing, and his own thin lips held a half smile. When he saw me on the sideline, he said a few more words to them and then walked toward me.

It was about four o'clock on a splendid Saturday afternoon in Denver. The two of us walked to his home. His nearby subdivision was lined with one-story brick houses, rather similar to one another, all with small front yards in various states of repair. A cluster of deep red geraniums gave color to one side of his neatly kept yard. At the other side, a short concrete driveway, no more than twenty feet long, led up to a garage attached to the house. Giant pylons carrying electrical wires stood behind the house, dwarfing us.

Ernst's wife, Anna, who was fifty and about Ernst's height, greeted us and led us inside to a tiny kitchen. Their refrigerator, which stood against the half wall separating the kitchen from the living room, featured a poster announcing a "Walk Against Hunger," with a black-and-white drawing of Jesus Christ alongside it. In the small living room, two old couches lined two of the walls. A television set and a bookcase crowded the other wall. The bookcase contained a three-volume collection of the classics and a book about the Bermuda triangle, among other works. No ornaments adorned the room.

Ernst, fifty-seven years old and a high school graduate, is a maintenance worker at the local high school. He first took the job in 1984. "It's mostly custodial work, and we also do setups for all the sports activities," he said in his rather high-pitched, raspy voice. "I'm in charge of the guys to make sure the sound system is ready, the field is in good shape, the markers are set up, you know. We each also have our regular area in the school to clean up on a nightly basis. I go in from two-thirty to eleven at night during the weekdays." He works with the students, too, he said, and his fondness for them was clear.

The Bartelles' oldest boy, Ernie, sixteen, who was returning from high school football practice, burst into the kitchen through the aluminum screen door. His brother, Hector, fourteen, ran in right behind him. They gave us a nod and a smile and introduced themselves. Then they bolted through the living room toward the back of the house. Anna stood and reached over to put her arm around Hector as he streaked by.

Like Ernst, Anna has a high school diploma. Employed in a local social service agency, she works nine to five, providing clients with information about available programs, managing the office, and doing casework for the mostly Hispanic clientele. She and Ernst, both Mexican-American, speak fluent Spanish. This is her fourth job in eight years. She returned to the work force at the age of forty-two. Because she had little seniority, she was laid off at each of her previous jobs after six months or a year as a result of staff reductions. Each layoff was a bitter experience, she said.

In 1989, Ernst earned $12,500. Anna, who had worked about half of that year at $5.50 an hour, made nearly $6,000, so together they earned about $18,500. This was a pretty typical year for the Bartelles, although their income has fluctuated depending upon how much of the year Anna was able to find work.

Ernst also volunteers at Anna's agency. Because their work schedules conflicted (Anna's jobs were all nine to five), Ernst and Anna were rarely able to see each other. On an ordinary day, Ernst left home at two in the afternoon to walk to the high school, and Anna didn't arrive home until after five. When Anna got the job at the social service agency, however, Ernst decided to start going in with her, volunteering three hours each morning at the agency. "Sometimes I get tired," Ernst said. "Eleven hours a day."

The Bartelles own a three-bedroom home, bought in 1978. The bedrooms are small and crowded, but Ernst says it is enough for them. In 1989, the Bartelles' housing costs averaged $495 a month, including utilities and telephone. "We've been lucky the roof never leaked," Anna said. "Everybody else's around here has." Ernst added, "It's a ten-year roof, and it's been over ten years. You just keep your fingers crossed." They spent about $75 a week for food. The cost of their 1981 Mercury, which had gone about 80,000 miles, came to nearly $2,400, including gas, insurance, repairs, taxes, and depreciation. "The car's falling apart," Ernst said. "Constant repairs, the clutch. They tell us we should get rid of the car, but we can't afford to buy another one." Ernst's job paid for most of his own medical insurance, but not for Anna's or the children's. Medical and dental insurance for the boys, which came out of Ernst's paycheck, cost about $1,600 in 1989 (Anna still was not covered). Total medical costs were nearly $2,100 for the year. The Bartelles spent roughly $600 on clothes for the four of them and $2,200 in federal income, Social Security, and state income taxes. These expenses amounted to about $17,100 in 1989. This left just $1,400 of the Bartelles' income to repair the house and furniture, buy appliances, purchase everyday household and personal items, go out to a movie or concert, or take a vacation. In fact, the Bartelles have gone out to eat or to the movies "only once in a blue moon," in Ernst's words. During the past eight years, the only vacations the Bartelles have had were a few weekend visits with one of Anna's sisters, who lives in a town about sixty miles away.

"It's been tough," Ernst said to me. "When I get my paycheck and my mortgage is due, after medical insurance and what the government takes, the whole thing doesn't cover my mortgage. The whole thing's gone. A couple of days ago, I just heard they want to raise the electricity rates another 13 percent. If they raise the rates, we're going to eat less. The only place we can cut back on is places like the food budget. Sometimes we've gone days just eating potatoes and eggs . . . sometimes just potatoes. When we buy food, sometimes, we don't have enough money to pay other bills. In other words, you rob Peter to pay Paul. You just juggle back and forth. We're always behind."

I wondered how the Bartelles clothed four people on $600 for the year. Ernst said, "We don't have any clothes, really. We just buy for the kids. The last time I bought clothes was at Montgomery Ward's. A couple of shirts and a couple of pants for work. Work clothes, really, is what it is. I still owe my sister $90. She bought them."

Anna said, "My sisters bring me things, that's how I manage. They have a lot of nice clothes. My sisters have provided me with nice clothes. They [my sisters] are about my size. I don't mind, because then I know I don't have to spend. I don't mind taking from my own family, but I wouldn't want to take from another person."

From time to time, Ernst and Anna have gotten other types of help from family members. One day, for example, the Bartelles received a check for $1,000 from one of Ernst's brothers. "He just sent it," Ernst said. "He didn't expect me to pay it back. I've got my pride. I won't ask. But if it's offered, I've taken it."

Ernie and Hector came back into the kitchen. Ernst gave

Ernie the keys to the car, and the two boys left. "We've been good parents," Ernst said. "We've tried to instill good values. We want the best for them. We're not drinkers or smokers. We've taught them to be very respectful of people. They don't join gangs or do drugs. Knock on wood that that never changes. But there's lots we haven't been able to do. I always wanted to take my kids places, take them around the country. Always wanted to expose them to things. I've wanted to take them to the national capital."

Anna broke in, "We haven't been able to furnish our home, make it nice. Look at those couches. Under the sheets they're worn, and they have holes in the seats. They're uncomfortable and ugly. The kids are going to be gone before it ever changes."

"And that's what hurts," Ernst said. "The kids know it. In their minds, when the kids are gone, it's going to be, 'Oh, the parents were always scratching and scraping.' That's a hell of a legacy to leave them. I'm hoping that someday I can quit my job here at school and get something rewarding that I like to do, and that's to help human services. I've put in applications all over," so far to no avail. "I'll tell you, I used to believe in God. Once I did. I don't know any more if there's a God. And if there is, I do know one thing: He doesn't love me."

Circumstances weren't always like this for Ernst and Anna Bartelle. In the last half of the 1970s and early 1980s, Ernst had been the area manager for six family-style restaurants owned by a national corporation. By 1982, his salary was almost $40,000, including commissions. Scheduled to work six days a week, he often worked on the seventh day, too. "I was always on call," Ernst said, "day and night."

The Bartelles purchased their home during those years. They also bought the Mercury new in 1981, having bought a Pontiac in 1978. They often went out in the evenings of his day off, and they took vacations. They could afford clothes for themselves and the children, and good furniture. They bought the better cuts of meat at the grocery. "Life was good," Anna said.

In 1983, on New Year's Day, Ernst learned that he would be laid off. "We just happened to find out by accident," Ernst recalled. One of his associates called and said he had heard that the corporation had sold the restaurants and that everyone was going to be let go. "It turned out it was true," Ernst continued. "We found out, 'Happy New Year. You don't have a job.' The first I heard anything in an official way, directly, was by memo. They informed me by memo a couple of weeks later, I think it was. The memo said that I was laid off, and the date of the layoff was the date I got the memo. That was my last day. We got no severance pay, no notice or anything. They were letting everyone go. I mean everyone." Another corporation had acquired the restaurants and replaced all the personnel. Ernst had turned fifty only five days earlier.

"I was devastated," Ernst said. "All of a sudden you've lost your job. Where do you go from there? You know if you're a young man you can always go looking. I knew I was going to have a hard time trying to get back into some other kind of business."

Anna remembered, "It was like the world suddenly collapsed, and I said, 'It's my turn now. I got to get out there and keep the family going.' So I went out looking for a job." Until 1980, Anna had worked as an admitting clerk in the county hospital. She had left her job in order to be home with the children, and thanks to Ernst's salary they did not need her paycheck. She had never stopped earning money, however. She started a private child care center in her home, and by 1983 five children were coming to her house from nine to five. She earned about $150 a week. "The living room was wall-to-wall baby cribs," Anna said. When she went back into the labor force in 1983, she soon got a new job as an insurance processor for a private hospital, earning $7 an hour.

Ernst was not as lucky. From 1967 to 1974, he had done social service work, eventually becoming director of the local Head Start program. In regard to his search for a job in 1983, Ernst said, "I applied for the state, the federal, the local, Catholic social programs, the aging, everything, because I had that kind of experience. I had social services experience, a lot of it. But I never got the jobs. I'm still not positive why. I was more experienced than a lot of them that got the jobs." It was an agonizing experience for him; both he and Anna believe that age discrimination kept him from getting the jobs.

Instead, while Anna went off to her job, Ernst kept the child care center going at home. "I baby-sat," he said. "I took over her job." Eventually, he found a job with the local school district as a truck driver's assistant in food services. He helped load the trucks, starting at five in the morning, and helped unload the food at various schools. It was a minimum-wage job. "After being turned down right and left for other positions, I wound up in food services, you know. I had to swallow my pride and work for minimum wage. It was very demeaning. I stayed at that job for about a year and then transferred over to the maintenance department, and I'm still working at maintenance." His six-year search for a better job has failed.

Anna said, "Things were out of control. I felt so sorry for Ernst. It's really a touchy subject for me to talk about, because I still cry about it. It was very sad for me to see a person of Ernst's capabilities going up there and being turned away time after time, and then he had to settle for a menial position. He was too overqualified or not qualified. He still applies for jobs and gets turned away."

"At one point," Ernst broke in, "the mortgage company wanted our house because we were behind on the payments. They finally went after it, but we were always able to borrow money to keep them off. [Simply keeping up with monthly expenses during the eight months he was laid off used up all his savings and forced him to borrow $4,000, mostly from other members of his family.] It's very scary because all of a sudden everybody knows who you are. We had people coming to our home to look it over, right here; we had to tell them literally to get away from our property. They were contacted through the mortgage company. They have a network identifying people who are potential home losers. We were scared. Very scared. Sometimes, it's very hard to explain, but sometimes I felt like I wish I was dead, you know. I got to the point that I wish I weren't here. Death would end it. Death is a way out. If I was by myself, I wouldn't give a shit. My life had become worthless."

Ernst continued, "There's been a lot of fighting between us. There's never enough money. If it weren't for potatoes at times, we'd starve. We're very proud people. We never asked for food stamps, you know. We've never asked for any public assistance except for unemployment. I took unemployment. That's very demeaning, and it was, but I needed the money. But as for welfare and food stamps, I never applied for them. I'm not afraid to work. I'm not too proud to take a job that doesn't cover my mortgage."

Anna said, "Ernst is a quiet person. He keeps things inside. But I voice my feelings. He took a lot of pressure from me. I blamed him, and I grew to hate him that he couldn't get a decent job, something more than he got. I detested him." Still tormented, she paused, near tears, before continuing, "I was at the point of breakdown. I felt like I was clawing for my life, fighting for my life and my family." She stopped again and then said, "You ever seen a hamster in a cage? It just runs and runs on its wheel and gets nowhere. That's what I feel like sometimes."

C h a p t e r   T h r e e

ECONOMIC
SELF-SUFFICIENCY IN
PRESENT-DAY AMERICA

When we reflect on the poor in America, we are apt to think of people who are unemployed or on welfare. Families such as the Lamberts and the Bartelles seldom come to mind. In part, this is because both are hardworking families with at least one full-time worker and often with two. In part, it is because the government does not define either family as poor. The incomes of both the Lamberts and the Bartelles are about 50 percent above the government's official poverty line. And it is also because neither family receives any public assistance. The Lamberts and the Bartelles appear, in all these respects, to be beyond poverty and able to make their own way.

The American ethos holds that hard work will enable people to provide adequately for themselves. If we are to learn whether this ethos reflects reality in America, we must determine whether families such as the Lamberts and the Bartelles have indeed attained a minimally adequate standard of living. To what degree are these families economically self-sufficient? This would seem to be a simple question to answer, yet the idea of self-sufficiency means different things to different people. Most would agree that persons unable to afford basic necessities on their own incomes are not self-sufficient. The disagreements arise when we go one step further and ask what is meant by "basic necessities." Which necessities are basic, and how much income do families need to afford them?

This question of definition may seem technical, but it is crucial. The answers to it will determine how many hard-working Americans are unable to obtain basic necessities and what kinds of experiences and backgrounds characterize such people. In turn, these answers will establish not only the size but also the nature and complexity of the problem of working poverty that the nation faces.

The government has attempted to measure poverty now for about thirty years with what has come to be called the official poverty line. Formulated at the birth of the War on Poverty, the measure starts with the idea that poverty signifies the inability of families to afford the basic necessities. The government chose an approach developed by Mollie Orshansky, then a little-noticed research analyst who was working for the Social Security Administration. Orshansky's own concern about the poor had deep personal roots, for she had come from a working-poor family. Although her father was a skilled tinsmith and repairman who nearly always had a job, she nevertheless recalls childhood days spent waiting in long lines to receive surplus food. "If I write about the poor," she said, "I don't need a good imagination—I have a good memory."[1] Orshansky had worked at the Department of Agriculture early in her career. She turned to studies of food budgets she knew of there that estimated the least amount of money required to purchase a diet that would meet minimal nutritional requirements. The studies adjusted this minimum cost for food to take into consideration both family size and the ages of family members, since children and even adults of different ages have somewhat different nutritional needs. Armed with the knowledge that the cost of food in the 1960s made up one-third of the budget for an average family, Orshansky set the poverty line for a household of given composition at three times the cost of the minimal food budget for that size household. The government adopted this formula as its measure of the official poverty line and thereafter updated it every year to take inflation into account. In 1970, the official poverty line for a family of four (two adults and two children) was $3,968; in 1980, it was $8,414; and in 1990, it stood at $13,360.

The word "poverty" has a broad reach, of course. To some, it means destitution, that is, living at a level of sheer physical survival, as people do today in many parts of the Third World. But ordinarily it means something more.[2] As originally conceived, the government's official poverty line signaled a standard higher than bare physical survival. Recall that in constructing the measure, Orshansky used the proportion of the family budget (one-third) that the *average* American family spent on food rather than the proportion that poor families spent on food.[3] The frame of reference originally was the budget and spending patterns not of the poorest families but of average Americans. That practice conveyed a definition of poverty that was tied to acceptable living standards.[4] People were impoverished, even if they were not starving or destitute, when they had incomes beneath the amount required to purchase basic necessities at the most frugal standard of an ordinary family. This approximates Orshansky's definition[5] and stays well within the confines of conventional meanings of the term.[6]

From the beginning, however, the government did not emphasize this concept of poverty, and it soon got lost. Orshansky had feared precisely this result. She believed that the government's formal adoption of the measure would "tend to freeze the poverty line despite changes in buying habits and changes in acceptable living standards" that would

take place in subsequent years.[7] The problem is that in
updating for inflation, the government in effect ignored the
concept of poverty that underlay the original measure. Spe-
cifically, the way the government calculated poverty meant
that the amount the average family spent on food continued
to be about one-third of the family budget, almost as if it
had been written in stone.[8] Over the years, though, changes
in the consumption patterns of the average American family
and the relatively rapid rise in the costs of other necessities,
such as housing and medical care, reduced the proportion
of the budget that the typical family spent on food and
increased the proportion it spent on other needs. By the early
1980s, for example, food had fallen to about one-fifth of
the cost of the average family budget in America, although
it remained at about one-third according to the poverty
measure. With the passage of time, then, the official poverty
line became ever more separated from its original mooring,
which, through the budget of the average family, had tied it
to minimally acceptable living standards. This, in turn, had
decisive implications for official reports about the total
number of Americans who were impoverished (reducing the
number significantly) and the kinds of Americans living in
poverty (far fewer working people were in poverty, for
example), which powerfully affected the government's conclusions and the nation's thinking about who the poor were.
This part of the story will begin to unfold in chapter 4.

The effect on the poverty line itself was dramatic. Had
the official poverty line first come into being in 1980, and
had it retained the approach to measuring poverty that was
originally used (with the cost of nutrition in 1980 taking
about one-fifth of the budget of the average American family),[9] the income necessary for a family of four to attain the
poverty line would have been around $13,300. This level of
income is more than 50 percent higher than the $8,414 that
the Census Bureau reported as the official poverty line for
1980. Calculated for 1990, when nutrition had fallen to about

one-sixth of the average family budget, the income needed for a family of four ($22,300) would have been 67 percent greater than the Census Bureau's official poverty line, which was $13,360. According to this revised calculation, which employs the same concept of poverty used at the start, the incomes of both the Lamberts and the Bartelles would be beneath the official poverty line instead of well above it.[10] What is more, having lost its connection with the original concept of poverty, and no alternative concept having been substituted, the government's official poverty line now had no solid tie to any concept of poverty.

The government should have had some inkling of the problem. One often hears that the federal government's left hand doesn't know what the right hand is doing. This applies, in some ways, to its measures of family budgets. For years, the government had two separate departments engaging in the development of these measures. The Census Bureau, in conjunction with the Office of Management and Budget, calculated the poverty line. Simultaneously, the Department of Labor compiled a series of other measures for family budgets that it called a "higher family budget," an "intermediate family budget," and a "lower family budget." The Department of Labor designed these budgets to detail consumption of all necessities, not just food, and to describe what it cost a family of four to live. The department compiled its family budgets for the last time in 1981. For that year, it found that the *minimum* amount a family of four needed to live on the lower budget was $15,323.[11] One might reasonably ask what could exist beneath the minimum amount required for a lower budget if not poverty, or something akin to it. Yet the amount was about 65 percent above the government's official poverty line. Something was wrong.[12]

Unbeknownst to the government, the Department of Labor's lower budget actually lent support to the poverty line as it had originally been measured. Indeed, the two were similar in concept, although few observers were aware of it. Both attempted to measure, in different ways, the minimum amount of income an ordinary family required to buy basic necessities. The two arrived at roughly similar answers, as well. Recall that the minimum income needed to attain the Department of Labor's last lower budget, in 1981, was $15,323. This was within 10 percent of the $14,374 figure for the official poverty line that would have resulted in 1981[13] had the government adhered to the concept and method that had been the bases of the original measure.[14]

In an assessment of what it takes for families to afford basic necessities, no less important than the ideas and calculations of governmental officials are the views and daily experiences of the public. Numerous surveys of Americans concerning these matters have been carried out over the years. Surveys, of course, must be used with caution, because the answers respondents give may be shaped by how they interpret the question. The individual's own income and life-style might well influence what he or she considers to be basic necessities or a minimally decent level of living. People with higher incomes are likely to believe that it takes a relatively high income to afford necessities and to live minimally decently. The possibility of this kind of problem is suggested by William Bennett's comment when he declined the offer to become national chairman of the Republican party at a salary of $125,000 a year: "I didn't agree to take a vow of poverty," he is reported to have said.[15] Consider, too, Robin Leach, star of television's "Lifestyles of the Rich and Famous," who was asked whether he considered himself to be a wealthy person. Responding that he did not, Leach said, "I have no servants. I do have a cleaning lady, like everyone else. I have no limo. In cities I usually hail a taxi like everyone else."[16] One person's luxuries may be another's necessities.

To avoid this problem, we might try a different strategy. We could ask respondents directly whether they have themselves experienced difficulty affording items generally considered to be basic necessities, such as food, clothing, and medical care. We can then connect the answers to the respondents' actual incomes and determine the level of income beneath which families report that they find it difficult to afford necessities. Unfortunately, this approach does not escape the problem. Although less obviously so, it still relies on the judgment of the respondents about what constitutes necessities. If respondents like fancy meals, they may eat out frequently. Respondents with these tastes who live on average incomes could easily answer that their income is insufficient for them to afford food. On the other hand, people with low incomes who eat frugally may believe that their incomes are sufficient to afford food without being aware that they may not be getting adequate nutrition.

Despite these shortcomings, survey results do tell us something important about the feelings of the public. Virtually every year going back to the 1950s, Gallup surveys have asked Americans what they consider the minimum amount of income a family of four needs to live in their communities. These polls reveal that the median response of the Americans surveyed never dropped beneath 140 percent of the official poverty line during the 1980s and reached a zenith of somewhat more than 160 percent of the official poverty line during the second half of the 1980s.[17] These responses approximate the income of the Department of Labor's lower budget and what the Census Bureau's official poverty line would have been if first constructed in the 1980s.

The same is true of the surveys that ask Americans about their ability to afford, food, clothing, and medical care throughout the year. In early 1984 and again in early 1987,[18] the Gallup organization asked Americans, "Have there been times during the last year when you did not have enough money to buy food your family needed?" The surveys asked this same question about clothing and medical care.

Comparing the respondents' answers with their yearly

Table 2
PROPORTIONS OF RESPONDENTS SAYING THAT
THEY WERE UNABLE TO AFFORD FOOD, CLOTHING,
OR MEDICAL CARE AT SOME POINT DURING THE
YEAR, 1984 AND 1987[a]

Family Income (in percentage of the official poverty line)	1984[b]	1987[b]
0–100	66.4	51.8
100–150	53.9	56.2
150–200	36.7	34.1
>200	17.7	17.6
Whole Population	30.8	26.8

[a] Tabulated from the tapes of the Gallup poll, January 27–30, 1984, and January 16–19, 1987.
[b] It may be better to view the measures, taken very early in the year, as measures for 1983–84 and 1986–87. The table thus uses the average of the poverty lines for each of the respective two years in calculating respondents' incomes as a percentage of the poverty line.

incomes and the size of their families reveals the percentage of the official poverty line at which a majority of respondents report that there were times during the year when they did not have enough money to afford one or more of these necessities. In both surveys, a majority of the families with incomes up through 150 percent of the official poverty line reported that they could not afford at least one of these basic items at some time during the year.[19] Only when family incomes rose above 150 percent of the official poverty line did a majority of respondents say that they were able to afford all three of these necessities throughout the year (see table 2).

This result parallels the experiences of the Lamberts and Bartelles, each of whom generally had an income hovering around 150 percent of the official poverty line.[20] Both families faced times when they could not afford necessities. Even after receiving financial assistance from others, the Bartelles sometimes had no money for food—they ate potatoes or potatoes and eggs for several days running—and the Lamberts could not afford school clothes for their children or dental care for themselves or their children.

We pointed out earlier that respondents' own incomes and life-styles might affect their views on the minimum income necessary to live, and this turns out to be so. On the average, higher-income respondents say that somewhat higher minimum incomes are required. However, even respondents whose family income lies at the lowest level—beneath the official poverty line—state that the minimum income necessary for a family of four to live in their communities stands at nearly 140 percent of the official poverty line.[21]

Not even residence in an urban or rural locale appears to change respondents' answers very much. In densely populated areas, something of a trade-off exists between housing and medical costs, which increase, and transportation costs, which often decrease because reliable mass transportation is more likely to become available. The evidence now available does not show, although it is often presumed otherwise, that urban-rural differences are strong or consistent enough to warrant making distinctions based on them in determining the income that the public feels is required for basic necessities. For example, the Gallup surveys of 1987 that asked Americans whether there were times during the year that they did not have the money to buy food, clothing, and medical care discovered little difference, on the average, in the responses of urban, suburban, and rural households. In all three locations, a majority of the households with incomes of up to 150 percent of the official poverty line reported that they ran short of money for one or more of these necessities during the year.[22]

The public's responses to questions about the minimum income necessary to live and the income required to afford food, clothing, and medical care throughout the year suggest that an income at or perhaps somewhat above 150 percent of the present official poverty line is required to achieve

Table 3

FOUR MEASURES OF THE INCOME REQUIRED FOR AMERICANS TO PURCHASE NECESSITIES, 1981–1990 (IN PERCENTAGE OF THE OFFICIAL POVERTY LINE)

	1981	1982	1983	1984	1985	1986	1987	1988	1989	1990
Official Poverty Line Recalculated for the 1980s by Means of the Original Measure[a]		150			156		168	169	172	167
Department of Labor's Lower Budget[b]	166									
Americans' Views on the Minimum Income Necessary to Live in Their Communities[ce]	164	160	154	151	146	163	160			
Income Level at Which a Majority of Americans Respond That They Sometimes Cannot Afford Food, Clothing, or Medical Care[de]				150			150			

[a] See the discussion on pages 33–35, above, for a description of the concept and measure that originally underlay the official poverty line. The expenditure weightings for food used to calculate the figures in the table are 20.4 percent for 1982, 18.8 percent for 1985, and 17.7 percent for 1987 and thereafter.

[b] Source: See note 11 of this chapter.

[c] Source: See note 17 of this chapter.

[d] Source: See table 2.

[e] These measures span two years; the measure for 1981, for example, combines 1980–81, using the average of the poverty lines for the two years. We do this because the surveys are taken in the early months of the year for which the measure is reported.

self-sufficiency. So does the Department of Labor's lower family budget. Even the concept of poverty that launched the official poverty line itself, when applied to the 1980s, leads to this same conclusion. The results of these various measures for the 1980s are found in table 3.

Unhappily, the measures do not themselves provide a consistent alternative measure of self-sufficiency. For 1981–82, the measures register at 150 percent, 160 percent, 164 percent, and 166 percent of the official poverty line. In 1987–

90, the available measures register at 150 percent, 160 percent, and 167 to 172 percent of the official poverty line. An examination of these results and those reported in the table for the other years indicates that the four measures usually register above 150 percent and rarely surpass 170 percent of the official poverty line.

To determine a threshold of self-sufficiency, we need to step beyond these measures and create an actual family budget designed to enable people to get all of the basic necessities at the lowest realistic cost (the appendix to this chapter contains the definition of basic necessities that is used here). The family budget listed below—which we call the economy budget—describes the income an American family of two adults and two children would normally need in 1990 (see table 4). It shows graphically why an income substantially above the official poverty line is necessary for families to be able to afford the basic necessities even when purchased at the lowest realistic cost.

The economy budget is stringent. For example, the expenses for food are only those allowed in the federal government's thrifty food budget, the same one that the government calculates to be the lowest with which a family can satisfy minimal nutritional needs. Some evidence indicates that the thrifty food budget may not cover the actual cost of food in low-income areas,[23] but we use it nevertheless. The housing portion of the economy budget is based on the level of rent for a two-bedroom unit defined by the federal government as a low-cost unit.[24] Table 4 and the footnotes to it summarize and explain the major items in the family economy budget.

To purchase the necessities found in this economy budget, a family of four in 1990 needed an income of about $20,700, which amounts to approximately 155 percent of the 1990 official poverty line of $13,360 for a family of four. This standard broadly coincides with the four governmental and public survey measures of self-sufficiency we reviewed, falling toward the lower end of their range.

Other considerations, too, suggest that this standard of self-sufficiency is by no means excessive. Because the economy budget is based on the expenses necessary to meet basic needs at the lowest realistic cost, its stringency is revealed as much by what it excludes as by what it includes.

What is it like to live on the economy budget? Members of families existing on the economy budget never go out to eat, for it is not included in the food budget; they never go out to a movie, concert, or ball game or indeed to any public or private establishment that charges admission, for there is no entertainment budget; they have no cable television, for the same reason; they never purchase alcohol or cigarettes; never take a vacation or holiday that involves any motel or hotel or, again, any meals out; never hire a baby-sitter or have any other paid child care; never give an allowance or other spending money to the children; never purchase any lessons or home-learning tools for the children; never buy books or records for the adults or children, or any toys, except in the small amounts available for birthday or Christmas presents ($50 per person over the year); never pay for a haircut; never buy a magazine; have no money for the feeding or veterinary care of any pets; and, never spend any money for preschool for the children, or educational trips for them away from home, or any summer camp or other activity with a fee.

Nor is this all. The budget allots no money either for any absence from work because of illness or to pay for emergencies or other unanticipated major expenses; no money to help other persons, such as an ill or elderly parent, or to buy life insurance or to pay interest on consumer-credit borrowing except for car financing; and no money for savings for college for the children or to support a pension for retirement other than Social Security.

This is not to say that a family living on the economy budget will never purchase any of these items. It is to say

Table 4

LOW ECONOMY BUDGET FOR A FAMILY OF TWO ADULTS AND TWO
CHILDREN, 1990

Food	(The lowest cost established by the federal government to provide minimally adequate nutrition for a family of four: $331 per month.)[1]	$ 3,972
Housing	(The rent level for a two-bedroom unit, including all utilities, defined by the federal government as a low-cost unit for its programs to assist low-income families, plus a telephone. The budget could comprise a monthly rent of $375, utility bills of $123, and a telephone bill of $18.)[2]	$ 6,192
Transportation	(Fifteen percent beneath the average annual cost for one automobile over 10 years and 100,000 miles, including depreciation, financing, fuel, tires, repairs, insurance, and taxes. The average American family of four has 2.1 cars rather than one. Nearly 90 percent of all households have at least one car.)[3]	$ 3,251
Medical	(The cost of medical care on average, for an American family of four)[4]	$ 1,568
Clothes	($250 per family member over the year)	$ 1,000
Personal[5]		$ 400
Incidentals[6]		$ 1,300
Tax	(Federal income, social security, state income)[7]	$ 2,975
		$20,658

1. In 1990, the cost of food for a family of four (two adults and two children) on the federal government's thrifty food plan is based on data provided by the Human Nutrition Information Service of the U.S. Department of Agriculture. For earlier figures, see Patricia Ruggles, *Drawing the Line* (Washington, D.C.: Urban Institute Press, 1990), p. 180.
2. The Department of Housing and Urban Development uses as its low-cost standard the 45th percentile of all two-bedroom rentals except new construction and public housing units. The figure for 1990 was $498 per month (for earlier figures, see Ruggles, *Drawing the Line*, p. 178), to which we added the cost of a telephone. Use of the 45th percentile of units seems appropriate both because some of the lowest-cost units are in rent-controlled apartments with long waiting lists (often they are rented by families with above-average incomes) and many other lowest-cost units are in dangerous neighborhoods that have high rates of violent crimes, areas that families may wish to avoid. See Christopher Jencks and Kathryn Edin, "The Real Welfare Problem," *American Prospect* (Spring 1990): 35. The housing cost that we use in the "economy budget," the 45th percentile, is an amount that may actually be spent for housing by many families with incomes at the official poverty line, equivalent to an income of $13,360 for a family of four in 1990, instead of the $20,658 of this economy budget (see note 32 below).
3. Bureau of the Census, *Statistical Abstract of the United States, 1990*, p. 609, table 1044.

The figure is 85 percent of the reported cost for 1988, adjusted to account for the rise in consumer prices in transportation in the years 1988–90. The average four-person household has 2.1 cars (ibid., p. 602, table 1028), and nearly 90 percent of all households have at least one car. See Robert Rector et al., "How Poor Are America's Poor," *Backgrounder*, Heritage Foundation, September 21, 1990, p. 8, table 4. For transportation price rises in the years 1988–90, see Council of Economic Advisers, *Economic Indicators* (Washington, D.C.: Government Printing Office, April 1991), p. 24.

4. Bureau of the Census *Statistical Abstract of the United States, 1990*, p. 99, table 151. The figure cited is the average medical care expense in 1987 of a four-person household, adjusted to account for inflation in medical care from 1987 to 1990. For medical care consumer price rises from 1987–90, see Council of Economic Advisers, *Economic Indicators* (April 1991), p. 24.

5. Personal includes soap, shampoo, toothpaste, toothbrushes, shaving cream and blades, feminine hygiene products, house cleansers, sponges, dish and wash towels, and other such items for a family of four for a year.

6. Incidentals include toys and presents ($200 per year to cover the four members of the family); repairs on household appliances, lamps, and furniture ($150 per year); purchase of used furniture, mattresses, bedding, towels, sheets ($300 per year); newspapers ($150 per year); school supplies ($100 per year for the two children); and such items as postage, dishes, utensils, glasses, napkins, stationery, and light bulbs.

7. Taxes include $1,075 for federal income tax, $1,510 for Social Security, and $390 for state income tax.

that in order to do so, such a family has to follow one of three alternatives. It has to borrow money, figure out a way to pay less for the necessities included in the economy budget, or find outside assistance. A family can borrow money, but there is no place in the budget for the repayment of debt (except for a car), so the repayment of loans requires the elimination of something else in the budget. The family might then turn to the second alternative: it can try to find a way to spend less for the necessities. Sometimes housing can be found at a lower price, although such housing may be in extremely poor condition.[25] As often the housing options available actually cost more than has been provided for in the budget.[26] Families may then decide to spend less on medical attention, a choice that many of them end up making.[27] They may also try to spend less on food, sometimes at the risk of sending their children to school hungry.[28] Or they can decide to go without automobile insurance. About two-thirds of the Americans who had no automobile insurance in 1987 lived in families with incomes beneath

$15,000.[29] They may also decide to forgo a telephone. Nearly one in seven households on an income between 125 and 150 percent of the official poverty line lacks a telephone, a rate four times greater than that of households living on the median household income.[30] Making these choices does free up money for purchases not contained in the economy budget. On the other hand, to forgo proper medical attention, to expose oneself to the dangers of driving without automobile insurance, and to have no telephone in a society dependent upon it is to live without necessities. One final alternative is to accept gifts or assistance from family, friends, church or synagogue, or some other source. This, the experiences of the Lamberts and Bartelles reveal, may be the only realistic choice.

Paul and Jane Lambert, heading a family of five, earned from about 150 percent to 160 percent of the poverty line, at the upper limit of the economy budget, for most of the period from 1984 to 1990. They did have some expenses not covered in the economy budget. Both Paul and Jane smoke. They also have two dogs. Although they live in a mobile home, their yearly housing costs are about $500 above the economy budget's expenses.[31] They also have two automobiles instead of one. But their car expenses, at $3,000, are about equal to those allowed in the economy budget (both cars are more than fifteen years old, both have gone more than 300,000 miles, and one of them frequently is out of repair). The closest public transportation to the Lamberts is more than a mile away and not terribly reliable. No other expense that they have goes beyond what is allowed in the economy budget. They do not drink, eat out, or go out to movies. They have bought no new clothes for themselves in many years. They have not been on a vacation away from home with their children in the past decade. They feel they cannot even afford the gas to go for a Sunday drive, and never do so. They have neither life insurance nor a pension for retirement. Juggling bills from week to week, they often make ends meet by getting assistance from others. They regularly depend upon outside assistance to pay for their food and shelter and to get clothes for their children. Even then, they cannot pay fully for necessities such as car repairs and medical or dental care.

The Bartelles are little different. Their income, which averages nearly 150 percent of the official poverty line, also hovers near the upper end of the economy budget. Like the Lamberts, the Bartelles have few expenses that go beyond the economy budget (they do have two dogs, and they spend $150 each summer to send both their children to day camp for a week). They, too, have been unable to afford to eat out, go to a movie, buy new clothes for themselves or their children, go on a vacation, buy life insurance, or do many of the other things that most American families take for granted. To make ends meet, the Bartelles get help from others to buy clothes both for themselves and for their children. Even then, money is sometimes so tight that they eat meagerly for several days running in order to have enough left to pay overdue mortgage, electricity, or gas bills. They do not have any money to spare either to replace worn furniture that has become bitterly embarrassing to them or to prepare to fix their roof.

In fact, the vast majority of American families living on incomes at the upper end of the economy budget share these experiences. Consider the costs for shelter. Housing expenses are so high that most Americans who live at the top end of the economy budget—155 percent of the official poverty line—cannot pay their present housing costs without scrimping on food, clothing, health care, or other necessities.[32] The Economic Policy Institute's detailed analysis of the American Housing Surveys reveals that about 90 percent of the families of four living at this income level in 1987 (equivalent then to about $18,000 for a family of four) did not, after spending only the minimal amounts alloted for food, medical, clothing, and other items on the economy budget, have enough money left to cover the rent or mortgage and utilities they had to pay for the shelter in which they lived.[33]

Housing is by no means the sole problem confronting these Americans. The economy budget presupposes that half or more of the household's medical insurance is paid by the employer. However, the actual experience of more than 40 percent of the households living at the top end of the economy budget is that the employer pays nothing for medical insurance.[34] As a result, these families either have no medical insurance whatsoever, not even Medicaid, or must purchase it on their own. Households that lack all insurance, as do about one-third of those at the upper end of the economy budget,[35] must pay all physician, hospital, and dental costs entirely out of pocket, appeal to the charity of the health profession, or go without.[36]

Not surprisingly, most households without medical insurance have substantially less access to medical care than does the average American family. Current research indicates that the adults in such households are 37 percent less likely to make any use of physicians' services during a year and 54 percent less likely to use inpatient hospital services than adults in households with medical insurance.[37] Even when they are admitted to a hospital, patients without private health insurance are apt to be given substantially less care. A 1985 study of more than one hundred hospitals found that inpatients who suffered from circulatory problems and "who were privately insured had an 80 percent greater chance of receiving angiography, a test for clogged arteries, than did those without insurance. The privately insured patients were 40 percent more likely to undergo coronary bypass surgery and 28 percent more likely to be given angioplasty, in which tiny balloons are used to open diseased arteries."[38] The medical establishment fully acknowledges the differential treatment. "The bottom line is clearly that the volume of care you get depends on your ability to pay," says James

S. Todd, executive vice-president of the American Medical Association.[39] Bruce Vladeck, president of the United Hospital Fund of New York City, concurs: "The poor can no longer expect the same standard of care as the middle class," he says. "Indigent patients at a New York public hospital will be moved to an eight-to-20 bed ward two days after surgery. They'd better hope that a family member shows up to assist in nursing."[40]

Even families with insurance may have large bills to pay. Full medical and dental insurance typically covers half the cost of dental surgery, for example. An operation to correct gum disease costing $3,000 would require a copayment of $1,500. Were the Lamberts or the Bartelles to face such an operation, it would consume nearly half of the family's annual food budget or two annual budgets for clothing for all members of the family. Or they could decide to decline the operation, which might result in the eventual loss of several teeth. These are the kinds of choices that families living on the Lamberts' and the Bartelles' income must make, even if they have insurance, when they confront the possibility of large medical bills.

Families attempting to get along on the economy budget face still other problems. Many of these families—indeed, many with even a somewhat higher income—reside in locales with schools whose students fall short of normal academic performance. Money is by no means the only factor in education, but few people would deny that it has an impact. Families that live on the economy budget are unable to afford property taxes, used to finance schools, at levels equal to the national average. Their children are also more likely to go to school ill prepared to learn, because they are hungry or sick or suffer from dental problems.[41] Moreover, their limited budgets do not permit them to give their children such advantages as preschool, home educational tools,[42] or educational trips and vacations. An exhaustive examination of the performance of America's high schools revealed that only

Table 5
DISTRIBUTION OF ANNUAL FAMILY INCOME FOR STUDENT BODIES OF
HIGH- AND LOW-PERFORMANCE SCHOOLS

Mean Annual Family Income	Low-Performance Schools	High-Performance Schools
Less than $10,000	1.1%	0.2%
$10,000–$14,999	21.1%	0.7%
$15,000–$19,999	34.8%	17.4%
$20,000–$24,999	32.2%	35.0%
$25,000–$29,999	9.8%	24.6%
More than $29,999	1.0%	22.1%
Mean Income	$18,934	$25,874

Source: John E. Chubb and Terry M. Moe, *Politics, Markets, and America's Schools* (Washington, D.C.: Brookings Institution, 1990), p. 107. Data are from 1980.

1 percent of the best schools in terms of the academic advancement made by their students had students whose parents' incomes averaged beneath $15,000 in 1980 (approximately 180 percent of the official poverty line for a family of four that year). By contrast, 22 percent of the high schools weakest in these terms had students whose parents' incomes averaged below $15,000. The ratio was precisely the reverse for students from families at the highest income level, above $30,000 (see table 5). A dramatic difference exists in the students' performance from the two kinds of schools. Students in the best high schools experienced an average rate of academic improvement from grades ten through twelve that was approximately three times greater than that found among students in the weakest schools.

Taken alone and in combination, these considerations about housing, medical care, and schooling portray the economic struggle facing families that are *not* officially poor. Had it only been retained, Mollie Orshansky's measure of poverty that launched the official poverty line would have revealed the hardship of these families. Families living on incomes of less than 155 percent of the official poverty line—

the top end of the economy budget—cannot afford basic necessities, even at the lowest realistic cost, unless they obtain substantial outside assistance. Even then many will fall short. Were these families to spend no more than the modest amounts the economy budget allots for the other necessities, more than four-fifths of them would have insufficient money left over to cover the cost of their housing. Since their access to medical insurance is often less than that of Americans who live beneath the official poverty line, they receive medical care far inferior to the average family's. Their children are twenty times more likely to attend a weak than a strong school. These daily experiences illustrate the predicaments that face Americans living on incomes lower than the economy budget, all of whom would be classified as poor today had the government not changed the original poverty index. For Americans with incomes beneath 155 percent of the official poverty line, life is grim. They are not making their own way. They are not self-sufficient.

As we define them, the "basic necessities" required to reach economic self-sufficiency are those items directly or indirectly necessary to sustain life and reasonable health, in both the short and the long term, plus a small amount for items one needs to express one's feelings to others and to participate at least minimally in the wider community. Directly necessary to sustain life and health are food, medical care, housing, clothing, and products to keep housing, clothing, and the family clean. People who are self-sufficient have, at a minimum, enough income to provide a diet for themselves and their families that meets the lowest federal government standard of nutritional adequacy. They are also able to afford housing that is neither dilapidated nor in a neighborhood known to be violent or especially dangerous. They are able to purchase medical care at a level equal to the average family's and the products necessary to keep their homes clean and persons healthy. They are able to buy enough clothing, generally secondhand, to keep themselves warm. Indirectly necessary for life and decent health now and in the long term are an education for one's children; transportation permitting one to be employed, do necessary shopping, and make other necessary trips; clothing adequate for employment and for one's children to attend school; and several smaller items, such as postage to pay bills. Finally, items necessary to express one's feelings to others and to be a part of rather than excluded from the wider community (beyond items already mentioned) are a telephone, an inexpensive television, a newspaper (also used to locate bargains and clip coupons), stationery, and the ability to give a few gifts to family members. This class of items makes up a very small portion (less than 3 percent) of the family's budget.[43]

AMERICA'S FAMILIES, AMERICAN WORKERS, AND ECONOMIC HARDSHIP: THE SCOPE OF THE PROBLEM

SANDRA BOLTON'S STORY

The wide array of families in America who fail to attain self-sufficiency, despite hard work, is astounding. The Lamberts and the Bartelles provide examples of families headed by married couples with children who are unable to make ends meet—one of them Anglo and the other Hispanic. Yet these families, though in trouble, are not the most likely ones to suffer the affliction of working poverty; the most likely are those headed by single parents, who must grapple with their harsh circumstances alone.

Sandra Bolton heads such a household. It would take a leap of imagination to fit the realities of Sandra's life into the American ethos that people who work hard and follow the rules will be able to make their own way. Sandra became a single parent following her divorce from her husband,

David, after six years of marriage and two children. In 1981, state Child Protective Services officials informed Sandra that the state would take her children if she did not leave David. Records showed that David had beaten her on several occasions, once breaking her jaw and another time knocking out a tooth. Child welfare officials considered him a threat to the children.

Today, Sandra works as a research associate at a medical center in the city of Phoenix. When I met her, the nine years since her divorce had taken an enormous toll on her, although one could hardly tell by her appearance. Her engaging face had the unlined complexion of a teenage girl, making her look much younger than her thirty-three years. Her thin frame held an elegant posture, and her dress was fashionable. As we conversed, she smiled often and talked easily, conveying the impression of a composed and happy person. It was only after speaking with Sandra over many hours that I learned the grim truth. The job of making a living and being a single parent had consumed everything she had to give and more.

In the process of the divorce, David left Sandra with nothing except the clothes belonging to her and the children, a little furniture and dishware, and a $125 car they had bought at a fire department auction several years earlier. Two weeks before the divorce became final, he piled most of the furniture and everything else that had any value into their pickup truck and drove off. She has neither seen him nor heard from him since. Nor have David's parents.

The first few months following the divorce were a nightmare, Sandra recalled. She said that she had feared David would return and brutalize her and the two children. Matt was then five and Todd was barely one. After graduating from high school and getting married to David, she had worked full-time in office jobs, but several months before the incident that precipitated the divorce she had quit her job to enter college. At the age of twenty-four, when the divorce occurred, she was a full-time student, single mother of two, unemployed, and virtually without funds. She was confused and disoriented, and very scared.

She applied for welfare but was told she would have to leave college. Instead, she decided to stay in school, dropping one course, and tried, somewhat naively, to earn her family's upkeep by giving piano lessons and selling blood. She took her two children with her to the state university and paid students to look after them while she was in classes. She soon found she was unable to earn enough money to keep up with the bills, however. Two days after the semester ended, she lost her apartment. "I was an hour away from being on the streets when a family at church said I could live with them," Sandra said. "They let me stay for two months."

While living with the Mattsons, Sandra got a full-time job at a medical center as a word processor, and Mrs. Mattson took care of the children. This enabled her to save enough money to get her own apartment.

For the next seven years, Sandra worked full-time at the medical center while taking one or two courses at night and during the summers. She maintained a high grade-point average and received tuition scholarships. In 1988, at thirty-one, Sandra graduated from college with honors in sociology. Raised in a small farming community, Sandra was only the fourth person from her high school graduating class of sixty to finish college.

Sandra began working at the medical center as a word processor in 1981 at an annual salary of $12,300. During the 1980s, she received three promotions. Her raises allowed her to keep a little ahead of the increases in the cost of living. By 1989, a year after her graduation from college, her salary had risen to $17,400. She and her two children lived in an apartment with two small bedrooms, a modest living room, and a kitchenette. The rent, utilities, and phone cost Sandra about $450 in a typical month ($5,400 a year). With two growing boys, her food bills came to about $300 a month ($3,600 a year). She has hypoglycemia, diagnosed when she was thirteen, and becomes too tired to function if she doesn't eat properly. "I use coupons for everything," she said. "We eat meat about twice a week, and I'm in a food-share program and save some money that way." Her company paid for her own medical and dental insurance, but insurance for her two children cost $85 a month. Doctor appointments, dental visits, and prescriptions not covered by insurance cost another $50 a month (the medical and dental bills totaled about $1,600 for the year). She had a 1985 Ford Escort with 117,000 miles on it, a car that she had bought used in 1987. The monthly loan payments ($110), insurance ($50), repairs ($30), and gas, oil, and tires ($40) amounted to $2,760 for the year. The repair bills would have been higher, Sandra said, except that her church had a single mothers' car clinic that paid for labor and sometimes also helped pay for parts. Clothes didn't cost Sandra much. "I buy just used stuff," she said. "I have a friend who works inside a major department store that donates to Goodwill and places like that. And she will call me and tell me the days that they're taking the clothes into stores and what store it is. And then I go there. I pay maybe seventy-five cents to two dollars for clothes." She got up and went into her bedroom, returning with a beautiful silk dress. "I got it for one dollar. It costs me more to get it dry-cleaned than it cost to buy it," she said with a good measure of pride, her face lit up in a warm smile. She bought mostly used clothes for her children, too. Only undergarments and shoes (which she says she can't find used) are bought new. She estimated that clothes for her and her children cost about $300 for the year.

These expenses came to $13,670. Federal income, Social Security, and state taxes and a retirement pension were another $3,150, for a total of $16,820. Sandra had to purchase personal items (such as soap, shampoo, toothpaste) and household items (such as napkins, dishes, glassware, towels, sheets, and blankets), buy or replace furniture, repair appliances, purchase school supplies for her children, and pay for other incidentals on the remaining $600 of her salary. This left no money for numerous other normal activities and needs such as entertainment, child care, or a vacation. Nor was any money left to meet an emergency.

Although in her eighth year of full-time employment, Sandra still didn't have the money to go to a movie and only rarely could pay for child care. She had not had a vacation since her divorce. To make ends meet, she had to turn to her church for help with her food bills, car repairs, and expenses for furniture. Her church has given her food certificates and helped with car repairs. She borrowed nearly every piece of furniture in her living room—two armchairs, a couch, and a table lamp—from members of her church. Besides these items, the living room contained only two end tables that Sandra had just purchased for five dollars each at a yard sale. "Until a week ago the lamp was on the floor," Sandra said. She had beds for her two children, borrowed from church members, but none for herself. She slept on a mattress on the floor. "That's my goal next year. I want to buy a bed," Sandra said.

Other people have helped her, too. Her boss paid half the cost of Matt's braces and retainer, and the insurance paid the other half. Her former in-laws have bought the children shoes and sneakers when Sandra did not have the money to pay for them. "My kids need shoes right now," she said. "One of them has a hole right in the back of his shoe, and it's raining today." Each year before the start of school, they also bought Sandra's children a set of new clothes.

From 1985 to 1987, Sandra tried to make ends meet by selling blood. She got nearly $1,000 a year donating blood. One day she fainted while at church, she said. The pastor then discovered that she was selling her blood to get enough money for food, and he began providing food certificates.

The certificates helped a little but not enough. Sandra says that there were times when she had only one dollar a day for her own food and ate soup and bread or crackers for a day or two in a row. "I call crackers and bread 'food stuffing,' " she said, "because they fill you up." She again tried to sell blood to get the money for food but was unable to do so. She had lost so much weight that she was beneath the required level for the center to take her blood. "I need to gain six pounds, but it's hard for me to do," she said.

She took on a second job, working two evenings a week at a library. This brought her a much valued $1,000 over the year. However, she was still at school trying to complete college. Coupled with her full-time job and her courses, the second job meant sixteen-hour days every weekday. She started at six in the morning feeding Matt and Todd, dealing with their other needs, and getting them off to grade school. She began work at eight. By the time she got home from her classes and library job, it was ten in the evening. The schedule kept her away from the children an unacceptable amount of time, causing her to feel like a negligent mother. "I was never there," Sandra said. She quit the second job after about a year. "I was so stressed out I was going crazy," she said.

When she graduated from college, Sandra put in applications for other full-time positions to try to find a better-paying job. She received offers to be a group therapist at a psychiatric institute, a social worker for a private agency, and a director of a youth center. "It was a depressing experience," Sandra said. "I learned after the application that the job as a social worker actually paid less than I was making at the time. The other jobs paid a little more, but had fewer medical benefits. So I've stayed where I am. I couldn't afford to move. I have a college degree with honors, but I've found many of the jobs just don't pay anything, not like what you're taught to believe."

Sandra knows other single mothers who have taken a different path. Some have gone on welfare. "Next door, there's a girl eighteen years old with two illegitimate children," Sandra said. "Her apartment is the same as mine, but it is paid for. She pays only twenty-two dollars a month. Her electric is paid for. She has practically all her food on food stamps paid for. She's living just about the same as I'm living, only she can stay home with her children. She watches soap operas all day. And I feel, sometimes, what the hell am I doing? I should stay home and be lazy. The women I know who do that look at me and say that I'm stupid for doing what I'm doing. 'You're the stupid one,' they say." Sandra began to cry. As she did, she picked up her cup (she owns no drinking glasses), took a sip of water, and then went on. "You try to do the responsible thing, and you're penalized, because the system we have right now doesn't provide you a way to make it. I mean, I work so hard. There's only so much a person can do."

Other women Sandra knows have taken up crime. One acquaintance, Barbara, quit a part-time job several years ago to deliver drugs a few times a week. Barbara believed it was completely safe and that there was no chance of her getting caught. She wasn't, and now she owns a brand-new seven-room house in a nearby town. "She paid for it completely with drug money," Sandra said. As she related this, she could barely conceal her deep bitterness, anger, and jealousy. They were unmistakable in her voice. Sandra told me that she herself had tried to buy a home for the past two years but had been unable to secure a loan.

"I know someone else," Sandra said, "who only has to deliver one package of drugs a week and make sure three or four cocaine vials get to somebody. Her kids always have new clothes. She has hundreds of dollars of spending money for her kids. I can't even put shoes on my kids' feet." She paused and then said, "It makes me think, if trafficking drugs is what you have to do to survive, I'm ready to sell drugs. I know it's dishonest, but I've done all the honest things, and look where it's gotten me. I can understand that people get so discouraged with the system that they're willing to traffic drugs. It's not honest, and I shouldn't even be in a situation where I have to consider that as an option."

She continued, "I consider myself an ethical and a moral person, and I would never do those things unless I was absolutely forced back into a corner with no other choice. And I see a society out there that just doesn't really offer realistic choices for good jobs. I've never had trouble getting a job or holding on to one. Jobs just don't pay good money. It forces you to think of alternative and not necessarily honest ways of earning money. It makes me angry. It makes me want to go out and do something drastic just so that people would hear my story, and maybe somebody would do something about it. But then I realize, you know, nobody cares. All I would do is get myself in trouble, and they'd say, 'See, I told you so; she's just like the all the rest.' "

Sandra has tried to resolve her inner torment through her belief in God, resulting sometimes in deeply conflicting feelings. "I have gone through several periods of severe depression," she said, "dealing with feelings of alienation, isolation, rejection by God, hunger, poverty, and just sheer anger at God for my situation. Although I know my situation is not His fault, I think, 'But He could stop this and change the situation.' That has caused me the most trouble. I have struggled continuously with this until the past year or so, when I finally reached a place of greater peace with Him, although I don't know why. I'm still poor, still hungry lots of the time, and still on the treadmill to oblivion, at least that's what it feels like. But, oddly enough, I have not lost hope. I have more faith in God than ever before that He will change the situation, that He has not utterly forsaken me and my children. I still have my periods of feeling like life isn't fair, but then I remind myself that God is just and that His justice will be there for me." She then paused, contemplatively, and added, "Some days, though, when it comes right down to it, I really don't know."

Sandra Bolton has not lost hope that a solution to her problem will come. Nor have the Lamberts or the Bartelles entirely lost hope. In conversations, they, too, expressed nothing so deeply as the desire to find a way to escape from their circumstances. They all share one view. Having worked hard and well in their present jobs and having tried unsuccessfully to get better-paying ones, they believe that improvement in their individual situation will require something reaching beyond the efforts they are personally capable of making.

THE SCOPE OF THE PROBLEM

Sandra Bolton, Paul and Jane Lambert, and Ernst and Anna Bartelle have something else in common. They believe they are not alone in their experience. They have little way of ascertaining how many, but they know that others live in similar circumstances. As Paul Lambert said, "I've got other friends like this. They're crazed because they can't make it."

How many others are there? We explore this question by examining the situation in 1989 and early 1990. The year 1989 marked the last calendar year of a remarkable economic recovery. Having begun in early 1983, the recovery entered its seventh successive year in 1989, making it the longest consecutive peacetime economic revival in the history of the nation. Our analysis, then, focuses on 1989, the culminating year of this historic recovery, and also on early 1990, before recession hit the nation in the late summer of that year and continued into 1991.

During 1989, 56 million Americans—22.8 percent of the American population—resided in households with incomes that could not realistically provide for basic necessities.[1] These households all lived on incomes below 155 percent of the official poverty line, all beneath the frugal economy budget we call the threshold of self-sufficiency.[2] After adjustments for family size, each of these Americans had an income equal to or less than the incomes of Paul and Jane Lambert, Ernst

Table 6
AMERICANS IN POVERTY ACCORDING TO THE OFFICIAL POVERTY MEASURE AND
THE ORIGINAL CONCEPT BEHIND THE OFFICIAL POVERTY MEASURE, SELECTED
YEARS, 1959–1989

	Official Poverty Measure		Original Poverty Concept	
	Number of Americans (in millions)	Percentage of Americans	Number of Americans (in millions)	Percentage of Americans
1959	39.5	22.4	39.5	22.4
1967	26.1	13.4	39.2	20.1
1972	24.5	11.9	35.6	17.3
1977	24.7	11.6	38.3	18.0
1982	34.4	15.0	58.5	25.5
1987	32.3	13.5	62.0	25.9
1989	31.5	12.8	62.8	25.6

Sources: Cited or calculated from U.S. Bureau of the Census, *Statistical Abstract of the United States* (Washington, D.C.: Government Printing Office), various years; Patricia Ruggles, *Drawing the Line: Alternative Poverty Measures and Their Implications for Public Policy* (Washington, D.C.: Urban Institute Press, 1990), p. 55, table 3.4; and the tapes of the Current Population Survey, March 1990.

and Anna Bartelle, and Sandra Bolton. At 56 million, the total number of Americans unable to afford basic necessities was nearly double the number of Americans—31.5 million—who the government's official poverty figures said lived in poverty in 1989.

Recall the observation in chapter 3 that, in its application of the official poverty measure over the years, the government lost sight of its original concept and, really, *any* concept of poverty. The poverty line was not measuring the same thing by the 1970s, let alone the 1980s or later, that it had been at the start. Reconnecting the official poverty line to its origins in order to apply it consistently over the years, we see a picture of poverty in America strikingly different from the one commonly accepted. Table 6 presents the nation's poverty levels as the official poverty line recorded them for selected years from 1959 through 1989. Alongside those figures, the table also presents the levels obtained by using the original concept behind the poverty line and applying it consistently throughout the three decades.

An application of the official measure without regard to conceptual consistency indicates that the proportion of Americans living in poverty declined by about two-fifths from 1959 through 1989, from 22.4 percent to 12.8 percent of the population. But a consistent application of the original tenets of the official poverty line discloses that the proportion of Americans living in poverty had not declined at all by the end of the three decades (see the right-hand side of table 6). The threshold of self-sufficiency, based on the economy budget, leads to broadly the same conclusion. In 1989, about 23 percent of the population was unable to afford basic necessities at the lowest realistic cost, as we have seen. As it was understood and measured at the very beginning, then, poverty remained about as widespread in America in 1989 as it had been at the start, in 1959. At that time, the breadth of poverty in America was considered so scandalous that a war to eliminate it was soon declared. In 1964, President Johnson said, "Our first objective is to free 30 million Americans from the prison of poverty." In 1989, there were more than 50 million Americans in that same prison.

The nation did make steady, if moderate, progress against poverty from 1959 to 1972, this despite the influx of new workers from the baby boom generation who began to flood the labor market after 1964. Yet poverty remained above 17 percent in 1972, still disturbingly high. The rate held steady through 1977, but thereafter soared to and somewhat beyond its level in 1959; it stayed at that level for the remainder of the 1980s. The extraordinary economic recovery of the 1980s barely put a dent in it.

Whom, then, did the recovery miss? Of the 56 million Americans with incomes beneath the threshold of self-sufficiency in 1989, 9 million lived in households headed by an ill or disabled worker. Nearly another nine million were older than sixty-five, or about three out of every ten of our senior citizens.[3] These two groups, combined, comprised 18 million people. This means that the remaining 38 million Americans resided in households whose incomes fell beneath self-sufficiency in 1989 *despite* their containing able-bodied adults of working age.

If the American ethos that economic opportunities are available to industrious workers is correct, characteristics such as idleness or laziness, inexperience and youth, and lack of education would provide logical explanations for the failure of these able-bodied Americans to achieve self-sufficiency. However, these traits do not describe Paul and Jane Lambert, Ernst and Anna Bartelle, and Sandra Bolton. In their worlds, hardworking, responsible Americans remain mired in economic privation.

They were far from alone. In March of 1990, when the nation was still four months from the end of its record-breaking recovery, 9.3 million workers in full-time jobs (10.3 percent of all full-time workers) found themselves in the company of the Lamberts, the Bartelles, and the Boltons.[4] The households of these workers, which contained 24 million persons, all had total incomes beneath the self-sufficiency threshold. The figures here refer only to full-time employees, not to part-time workers unable to find adequate full-time employment. We will return in chapter 6 to a more detailed examination of the situations and experiences of these other workers and their families, who bring the total number of working Americans living beneath self-sufficiency to nearly 30 million.

Because of factors like illness, layoffs, and business closings and relocations, however, workers are sometimes unable to work full-time the whole year. Both Paul and Ernst found themselves in this circumstance at times. In 1983, Ernst was laid off and became unemployed for four months because of a company takeover in which all the employees were let go. Paul, too, left a job in 1989 because of poor working conditions and then was laid off another in 1990 when the company went bankrupt. Ernst's wife, Anna, lost two jobs between 1988 and 1990 because of cutbacks in personnel in the companies that employed her.

A stricter standard for examining self-sufficiency would involve looking solely at "fully employed" workers—those employed full-time for the entire year. This was the Lamberts', Bartelles', and Boltons' usual situation. Even by this standard, 5.9 million American workers (7.4 percent of all fully employed Americans) worked full-time the whole year during 1989 and yet lived beneath the threshold of self-sufficiency. The households of these fully employed workers contained 18 million Americans. This number is the equivalent of every man, woman, and child living in the eleven largest cities on the nation's two coasts—New York City, Los Angeles, Philadelphia, San Diego, San Jose, Baltimore, San Francisco, Jacksonville, Washington, D.C., Boston, and Seattle. That is four to five times more Americans than are often defined to be in the "underclass," and more than half again as many people as were on welfare at any one time that year.[5] About one in three of the workers lived beneath the official poverty line; as a consequence, people who think only of the official poverty line as the standard of poverty would fail to perceive the economic hardship that the remaining two-thirds endured.

The heads of these families were employed in a wide variety of occupations. During the concluding year of the prosperous 1980s recovery, more than 10 percent of America's machine operators who worked full-time the entire year lived in households whose incomes fell beneath self-sufficiency.[6] The same was true for America's fabricators and assemblers, health service workers, farmers and farm operators, building laborers, freight and material handlers, repair service workers, textile and apparel workers, social service workers, carpenters, retail workers, cleaners, and personal service workers. More than one in five of all fully employed workers in the United States held jobs in these occupations. Also living beneath economic self-sufficiency in 1989 despite full-time work for the entire year were 9 percent of all transportation workers and furniture makers, 8 percent of the precision product workers and workers in construction trades, 7 percent of the mechanics, 6 percent of the production testers and inspectors, and 5 percent of all supervisors and proprietors and protective service workers.

They could have lived down the street or across town, and often we would have been unaware of their existence. A bitter irony of this kind came to light in 1988 when the presidential candidate George Bush made patriotism and the American flag into an election issue. In an effort to portray himself as more patriotic than his opponent, Michael Dukakis, Bush appeared at a factory in Bloomfield, New Jersey, that made American flags. All the networks and major print media organizations covered his visit. At the factory, Bush expressed his devotion to the flag and his admiration for the workers who made it. He remarked on the newfound pride that had arisen in America during the Reagan-Bush administration—a pride, he said, that had sparked the extraordinary American economic revival.[7] The crowd cheered. Hundreds waved flags. What remained unnoticed in Bush's oratory were the wages of the workers who made the flags. They were getting between $3.35 and $6.50 an hour,[8] an average of $4.95 an hour. At these wages, the earnings of even two workers, both employed full-time over the entire year, would barely permit a family with two children to lift itself to the edge of self-sufficiency. One of the workers at the plant said, "We're begging, just begging."[9]

That the plight of these workers has gone mostly unnoticed is not terribly surprising. American workers who are fully employed with incomes beneath self-sufficiency tend to be at the margins of the political process as they are at the margins of the economy. They belong to fewer community organizations than do families living on higher incomes.

Employed heads of more than 40 percent of the households whose incomes fall beneath self-sufficiency do not belong to any community organization. By contrast, the heads of more than 80 percent of the families living above the self-sufficiency threshold belong to one or more community organizations.[10] They are less directly involved in the political process, too. Fewer of them register to vote, fewer who are registered do vote, fewer contribute money to political candidates, and fewer join political organizations.[11] In 1972, the Supreme Court acknowledged the political marginality of poor Americans. In a moving statement on behalf of the Court, Justice Lewis Powell wrote, "Empirical examination might well buttress an argument that the ill-fed, ill-clothed, and ill-housed are among the most ineffective participants in the political process, and that they derive the least enjoyment from the benefits of the First Amendment."[12]

It is likely that a series of factors helps explain the low participation and political marginality of these families. For one, their economic plight may produce the feeling that they are not fully a part of the community, even though they are full-time workers. They also lack the economic resources and possibly the confidence usually helpful to involvement in political and social life. Then, too, their preoccupation with survival undoubtedly leaves many of them little time or energy for other activities. More than half the heads of families with an income beneath self-sufficiency, like that of families beneath the official poverty line, say that they worry all or most of the time about whether they will have enough money to pay the bills. Fewer than one-quarter of the heads of other American households express this level of concern.[13]

Poor workers resemble the young in their low levels of political participation. It is indeed tempting to believe that the majority of Americans who find themselves fully employed and yet living beneath self-sufficiency are fairly young, perhaps in their teens or twenties. One might hope that as these

Table 7

AGE, EDUCATION, AND PERCENTAGE OF FULLY EMPLOYED WORKERS WHO
LIVE BENEATH ECONOMIC SELF-SUFFICIENCY, 1989

	Age					All Workers
	16–24	25–34	35–44	45–54	55–64	
Less than High School Degree	32.9	27.8	22.2	14.3	13.0	20.5
High School Degree	11.8	11.0	8.2	5.1	3.9	8.3
One to Two Years beyond High School	8.1	5.6	5.3	4.0	3.4	5.4
Three Years beyond High School	7.6	3.8	4.7	2.5	2.6	4.6
College Graduate	4.9	2.1	2.1	1.1	1.3	2.1
All Workers	12.4	8.4	6.5	5.0	5.0	7.4

Source: Compiled from the Current Population Survey tapes, March 1990.

workers age and get more employment experience, their incomes will increase, eventually enabling them and their families to reach self-sufficiency. However, Ernst Bartelle, fifty-seven, and Paul Lambert, thirty-nine, work full-time the whole year and yet live beneath the threshold of self-sufficiency. The failure of year-round full-time work to yield incomes necessary for self-sufficiency affects Americans in every age group. In fact, nearly half of all workers who fail to achieve self-sufficiency despite year-round full-time employment are older than thirty-five.

It is true that the probability that a fully employed worker will fall beneath self-sufficiency declines with age and that age is an important predictor, as table 7 shows. The rate of economic insufficiency shrinks from 12.4 percent for 16-to 24-year-olds to 5.0 percent for 55-to 64-year-olds. Nevertheless, even when age is controlled for, much of the problem remains. Fully employed Americans older than 35, for example, fail to reach self-sufficiency at a rate averaging 5.6 percent. If all fully employed Americans under 35 were to have the same 5.6 percent rate of economic insufficiency as those over 35, more than 4 million fully employed workers would still be living beneath self-sufficiency, not even one-third fewer than exist now.[14]

Yet more surprisingly, the same is true for education. America provides free universal education through high school. Beyond that, education is neither free nor open to everyone. Perhaps partly because higher education usually involves some financial cost and some academic selectivity, about half of the American workers, including those now in their twenties, have no formal education beyond high school. Fewer than one-quarter of all American adults have completed a college degree.[15] The high school diploma remains the predominant terminal degree for all age groups.

The news today is full of alarming stories about the numbers of students who drop out of high school. It would be no surprise to discover that these high school dropouts—having failed to take advantage of an opportunity open to all and widely thought to be essential to making one's way—face substantial economic difficulties. These Americans do indeed face difficulties, even when they are fully employed. In 1989, about one-fifth (20.5 percent) of all fully employed American workers without a high school degree lived in families unable to achieve self-sufficiency. Education, like age, is a powerful predictor of working poverty.

Nevertheless, completion of high school by no means ensured that fully employed workers would be self-sufficient. The Lamberts and the Bartelles, for example, all earned a high school diploma, and Sandra Bolton had gone beyond that. In 1989, of all fully employed workers regardless of age who had earned a high school diploma, 8.3 percent lived in households that fell beneath the threshold of self-sufficiency (see table 7), a rate *greater* than the overall national rate of 7.4 percent. This is to say that achieving the highest level of education that is both free and open to all and that about half the population has not exceeded would still leave large numbers of Americans in working poverty and the nation with a significant problem to resolve.[16]

It is not merely the younger fully employed high school graduates who are in this situation but the middle-aged ones as well. For example, among workers aged thirty-five to forty-four, many of whom are in the middle or latter years of raising children, 8.2 percent who had a high school degree and held year-round full-time jobs lived in families with incomes below self-sufficiency (see table 7). Barely one-third fewer of the fully employed workers from this age group found themselves in the same circumstance even if they had completed up to two years of college.

In 1989, after seven consecutive years of nationwide economic growth, nearly six million American workers, with eighteen million Americans living in their families, were employed full-time the entire year and yet failed to reach self-sufficiency.[17] Their experience stands in sharp contrast with the belief that all hardworking people will be able to make their own way. The majority of them are neither young nor high school dropouts. That so many fully employed Americans could not attain self-sufficiency at a time of sustained economic growth suggests that something thought to be essential to the idea of America has gone wrong.

Our focus on fully employed workers whose families end up living beneath self-sufficiency, in fact, has highlighted only one part of a far larger problem, as our earlier descriptions of low-paying occupations may have suggested. The failure of families with full-time workers to attain self-sufficiency occurs in the context of low wages, a condition that penetrates deeply into the American economy and family life. In 1989, nearly 40 percent of all year-round full-time workers earned less than it took to keep a family of four out of poverty. They totaled 31 million workers. More than one in every five full-time workers (18.4 million) earned under three-quarters of that amount. It is impossible to calculate precisely how low wages shape workers' decisions about such matters as whether to marry, whether to have children, and how many adults to place in the work force. It would seem enough to say that building the American family sometimes portrayed as a model—two parents and two children, with one parent employed and the other at home, particularly when the children are young—is not an alternative open to large numbers of the full-time work force in America, unless they stand ready to be poor. The consequence is that many millions of working families face a Hobson's choice. They can place one worker in the labor force and live beneath self-sufficiency, or they can place two workers in the labor force and forgo having an adult at home with the children.[18] Among dual-adult families that live in poverty despite having a full-time worker, more than half either put a second adult in the labor force or have children beneath the age of six. The struggle of Ernst and Anna Bartelle and Paul and Jane Lambert vividly illustrates that even the earnings of two working adults in a family, both employed full-time, can easily fall short.

WORKING AMERICANS AND ECONOMIC HARDSHIP: THE COMPLEXITY OF THE PROBLEM

Three explanations for working poverty in America are commonly advanced. Each provides the intellectual underpinning for a policy approach to address the problem. As we will see, however, the policies have not been able to penetrate much beneath the surface. Nor can they prove effective, for their underlying explanations of working poverty are inadequate, failing to identify the roots of the problem.

One widely cited explanation is that lower-grade job opportunities for both minorities and women, and the resulting lack of decent pay, constitute a significant cause of working poverty. A chief competing argument holds that working poverty exists among American workers regardless of race, gender, and formal education when workers have weak basic educational skills. Poor-quality education lies at the heart of working poverty, according to this view. A third approach claims that working poverty results from the growing proportion of low-paying jobs in our economy, brought on by the erosion of the nation's industrial base and its loss of competitive power in the global market during the past thirty years, an agonizing process in which millions of decent-paying jobs disappeared.

All these explanations deserve attention. This is not simply because each stands behind conventional images of the poor—that the poor in America are mostly single female parents, minorities, poorly educated workers, or workers who have lost well-paying jobs in aging manufacturing industries. It is also because these same theories provide the foundation for many of the leading strategies for attacking working poverty in America. Debate centers on proposals to end employment discrimination and provide equal job opportunities, improve the quality of education and worker skills as well as reduce the rate of school dropouts, and upgrade the nation's industrial competitiveness and job-creating power, particularly in industries, such as manufacturing, that carry the nation's fortunes in international trade.

Faith in the American ethos that opportunity should exist for all makes it tempting to believe that effective implementation of one or more of these strategies can successfully combat working poverty. On the other hand, if the factors at the foundation of these theories cannot account for a large percentage of those living in working poverty—if the nature of the problem differs from conventional understandings—then strategies derived from them will fail a large number of workers who are now unable to attain self-sufficiency despite year-round full-time employment.

RACE, GENDER, ACADEMIC SKILLS, AND WORKING POVERTY

Sandra Bolton's having to sell her blood in order to make ends meet though she held a full-time job can only make

Table 8

RACE, GENDER, EDUCATION, AND THE PERCENTAGE OF FULLY EMPLOYED HEADS OF HOUSEHOLD WHO LIVE BENEATH ECONOMIC SELF-SUFFICIENCY, 1989* (IN PERCENTAGES)

		Level of Education				
Total	Race and Gender	Below High School	High School	One to Two Years beyond High School	Three Years beyond High School	College Graduate
6.4	White Male	19.0	7.1	4.9	3.8	1.9
11.5	Black Male	23.7	10.3	8.0	5.8	5.3
10.2	White Female	29.5	13.1	9.4	7.0	2.8
21.8	Black Female	38.7	25.7	16.8	9.9	6.5

* The table covers households both with and without children.

Source: Figures are compiled from the Current Population Survey tapes, March 1990.

one wonder whether she has not suffered from consignment to a world of pink-collar desperation where the kinds of jobs available to workers of her gender are disproportionately low-wage and dead-end ones. One must ask, too, whether Ernst Bartelle's inability to find a better job, despite all his efforts, might not be related to some degree to his minority status.

Minority status and gender are indeed important[1] (with respect to minority status, we will henceforth focus on the largest minority group in the nation, the black population). Fully employed blacks and females fall beneath self-sufficiency much more often than do white males, as table 8 shows. About 22 percent of the black females, 12 percent of the black males, and 10 percent of the white females, though fully employed, failed to achieve self-sufficiency in 1989, compared with 6.4 percent of the white males. It is noteworthy that no matter the level of the workers' educational credentials, race and gender nearly always made some difference in the rate of economic insufficiency.

Yet differences in income by race or gender cannot explain Paul Lambert's battle against economic marginalization. His broken-down car and inability to afford clothes for his children are painful symbols of the reality of low wages in the lives of fully employed white males in America, not just in those of minorities and women. Because they are so dominant in the labor force, in fact, white males head the largest group of working-poor households. As a result, not even the complete elimination of all differences in pay between the races and genders, important as they are, would penetrate deeply into the problem of working poverty. That is, if America somehow became a place where race and gender had no connection whatever with working poverty, the numbers of Americans who work full-time year-round and yet remain in poverty would decline only moderately. Suppose the overall rates of economic insufficiency among minorities and females were effectively reduced to the rate for white males; that is, assume the rate of economic insufficiency for all groups of workers became exactly the 6.4 percent rate that white males experience. About five million fully employed American workers would then remain beneath self-sufficiency, which is still approximately 85 percent of what we have now.[2] In a just society, the elimination of economic differences that exist between minorities and whites and between males and females is critical whenever they are the result of discrimination, but their removal would still leave much of the problem of working poverty well in place.[3]

Some observers believe that another factor is at play here, more important than whether workers are white or minority, male or female, or even whether or not they have graduated from high school. This concerns the quality of education and skills that workers have.[4] Workers who have gotten a formal education through high school or perhaps even somewhat beyond might have difficulty finding decent-paying jobs if the schools they attended were weak and the skills they received were of poor quality. Secretary of Labor Lynn Martin and a former secretary, William E. Brock, chairs of the Department of Labor's Commission on Achieving Necessary Skills, told the nation that too many Americans today "leave school without the knowledge or foundation required to find and hold a good job. . . . Low skills lead to low wages and low profits. Many of these people will never be able to earn a decent living."[5] One hears stories of people who graduate from high school without being able to multiply anything more than single-digit numbers or read beyond the level of a fifth- or sixth-grader. Some illiterate students have made it through high school, unable to read so much as the directions on a bottle of medicine or the forms to get a driver's license. Among such workers, only lucky exceptions could be expected to hold down decent-paying jobs.

Americans have long had faith in the power of education and so tend to believe that many doors in life will be open to individuals who have gotten themselves a quality education. Popular books and movies, such as *Lean on Me* and *Stand and Deliver,* carry this message. They immortalize the true stories of hard-driving principals, such as Joe Clark of Paterson, New Jersey, and brilliant teachers, such as Jaime Escalante of Los Angeles, who have taken failing schools and students from poor neighborhoods and transformed them into models of achievement and success. The moral of these inspirational stories is the same as the premise of the American ethos: failure results among individuals who have low expectations, little pride, and an unwillingness to work hard. By taking responsibility for their actions, these stories tell us, most students and school officials with high expectations can overcome failure. An additional implication of the message is that students who succeed in school will be able to succeed in life.

Yet Sandra Bolton had an outstanding school record, ultimately graduating from college with honors. Less is known of Paul Lambert's and Ernst Bartelle's educational performance other than that they graduated from high school, but both are bright, talented, articulate people. Paul demonstrated his abilities at Andrews' Electronics, where his boss described his performance as exceptional and said that he had resolved many recurring problems and inadequacies since his arrival at the firm. Ernst had successfully managed six restaurants prior to the buyout of the company for which he worked.

Evidence of a link between the quality of educational skills of American workers and the economic success they achieve is difficult to find. Few nationwide surveys of workers during the 1980s tested academic skills. One important exception is the National Longitudinal Survey of Youth, conducted by the National Opinion Research Center of the University of Chicago. This survey gave the Armed Forces Qualifications Test (AFQT) in 1981 to each of its approximately twelve thousand respondents, who were then aged seventeen to twenty-five. The AFQT includes a battery of separate subtests of academic skills covering word knowledge, paragraph comprehension, arithmetical reasoning, and numerical operations. We divide the respondents into two groups: workers with "lower academic skills" (those whose scores on the AFQT subtests are in the bottom half of the respondents) and workers with "higher academic skills" (those whose scores on the AFQT are in the top half of the respondents).[6]

To what degree does the level of academic skills, as measured by the AFQT, affect the earnings levels of America's fully employed workers? To answer this question, we examine earnings levels for the individual worker rather than the total income of the worker's family (which often includes more than one worker). This enables us to focus on the effect a quality education has on the wages that individual workers are able to earn. We define a low wage or earnings level for a year-round full-time worker as three-quarters of the income needed to reach economic self-sufficiency for a family of three.[7] For 1986, the last year of the National Longitudinal Survey available to us, this amounted for a fully employed worker to earnings over a year not exceeding

$10,500.[8] In that year, the oldest respondents in the survey had reached the ages of twenty-six to thirty, the family-building years for many Americans. The majority of them had been out of school for about a decade. Our examination centers on this group of workers.

An analysis of the data reveals that the quality of academic skills of fully employed workers has a significant influence on earnings. Consider simply the experiences of male workers. In 1986, fully employed male workers with low academic skills were twice as likely, or more, to have jobs with low earnings (less than $10,500 a year) than were workers with high academic skills, regardless of their level of formal education or race (see table 9). So skill, as opposed to credentials, mattered. Academic skill was of such importance, indeed, that among the workers with high academic skills race no longer had much of an effect on the earnings of workers. The incidence of low earnings was approximately the same among blacks as among whites.[9] On the other hand, race still exerted an important influence on the earnings of fully employed workers with low academic skills and no more than a high school education, characteristics that embrace about half the black workers and a sizable minority of white workers; here differences along racial lines continued to be manifest.

Table 9 contains another crucial finding, however. The problem of fully employed workers earning low wages was widespread, by no means confined to workers with below-average academic skills. Even among fully employed white male workers with a high school education and above-average academic skills, 11.8 percent held jobs paying less than $10,500 in 1986. Indeed, 9.3 percent of the fully employed white male workers with above-average academic skills who had completed at least some college education had earnings below this level.

Perhaps some of these workers had not been steady job-holders over the years. The National Longitudinal Survey

Table 9

FULLY EMPLOYED MALES AGED 26–30 WITH EARNINGS BENEATH ECONOMIC
SELF-SUFFICIENCY,* 1986, BY RACE, EDUCATION, AND ACADEMIC SKILLS
(IN PERCENTAGES)

Race and Academic Skill Level	Below High School	Completed High School	Completed at Least Some College
White, Low	33.2	25.3	22.6
White, High	13.7	11.8	9.3
Black, Low	48.3	35.6	23.7
Black, High	**	13.1	10.6

*Beneath three-quarters of the income needed for economic self-sufficiency for a family of
three.
**N is below 25.
Source: Figures are compiled from the National Longitudinal Survey of Youth tapes.

enables us to look at the employment experiences of the same
respondents over a number of years. Doing so discloses that
the problem of low earnings among American workers
extends even to workers with steady year-round full-time
employment year after year. This is especially true for blacks
(as table 10 shows). Among workers with low academic skills
who had not gone beyond high school, black males who
were employed full-time throughout all four years from
1983–86 fared considerably worse than did white males with
equivalent education and academic skills. At the lower edu-
cational-skill levels, once more, race made an important difference. Yet, even among white male workers with a high
school education and above-average academic skills, 10.3
percent who were employed full-time throughout the four
years had jobs with low earnings at least half of those years.
So did 8.1 percent of the white males with above-average
academic skills who had gone beyond high school and
obtained some college education. Being a white male with a
high school education or some college training, above-average academic skills, and a four-year history of steady full-
time employment was no guarantee against working for low
pay. If America were able to eliminate the pay differential

Table 10
MALES AGED 26–30 IN 1986 WHO WERE CONTINUOUSLY FULLY EMPLOYED
FROM 1983 TO 1986 WITH EARNINGS BENEATH ECONOMIC SELF-SUFFICIENCY*
AT LEAST HALF OF THOSE YEARS (IN PERCENTAGES)

Race and Academic Skill Level	Below High School	Completed High School	Completed at Least Some College
White, Low	19.8	13.9	**
White, High	**	10.3	8.1
Black, Low	40.6	24.8	6.3
Black, High	**	**	0.0

* Beneath three-quarters of the income needed for economic self-sufficiency for a family of three.
** N is below 25.
Source: Figures are compiled from the National Longitudinal Survey of Youth tapes.

between blacks and whites and between men and women, achieve a high school dropout rate of zero, and raise everyone's academic skills to the level of those of the upper half of the population (idealistic goals even by the standards of the most ambitious reform proposals), the problem of low-wage employment, unhappily, would not be solved.

THE DECLINE IN MANUFACTURING

Continuously employed white men who hold high school degrees or have some college and who also have above-average academic skills transcend conventional images of workers at the lowest end of the wage scale. That so many of these workers, and millions of others, are in low-wage jobs stands at odds with the claim sometimes heard that plenty of decent-paying jobs are available. They go unfilled, it is said, because workers do not have the necessary education and training for them. Unfortunately, the government does not undertake national surveys to tabulate the number of jobs that remain unfilled for weeks or months at a time. Such tabulations are available on full-time employment, part-time employment, unemployment, length of unemployment, reasons for unemployment, and thousands of other categories across the entire range of business and economic activity. But the government provides no similar statistics on the total number of unfilled jobs and the length of time the jobs have gone unfilled or the pay of the jobs. As a result, evidence on the subject is largely anecdotal. Such statistics are needed, for it seems highly unlikely that heads of families, many of them educationally skilled, would choose to work full-time at low wages and continue to live in economic distress if a large number of decent-paying jobs for which they could be trained were available and going begging for long.

That educationally skilled workers—and many others, too—hold on to low-wage jobs instead suggests that most of them have no opportunity to do otherwise, even if they are all willing to move. They live in an economy where large numbers of jobs, even for fully employed workers, pay very little, often far beneath the amount needed to support a family.

Low-wage employment riddles the economy. Workers in eleven million jobs providing year-round full-time employment in 1989 earned less than $11,500 for the year.[10] These wages come only to three-quarters the income a family of *three* needed to reach self-sufficiency during that year. One in every seven (14.2 percent) of all jobs for fully employed workers in 1989 offered this level of pay, or lower. Despite the low pay, nearly one million workers holding the jobs had earned a *college* degree; more than 2.5 million of them had gotten at least a year of education beyond high school, just about matching the number of high school dropouts holding these jobs. Conditions were still worse for workers in families of four. Eighteen million jobs available to fully employed workers paid less than three-quarters of the income a family of four needs to attain self-sufficiency. This amounted to 23 percent of all the nation's year-round full-time jobs in 1989. With so many steady full-time jobs paying well beneath self-sufficiency for families of three or four, it is no surprise that nearly six million fully employed workers were in fact unable to attain self-sufficiency in 1989 and that they came from a wide spectrum of backgrounds.

What can account for the existence of these jobs? Unhappily, conventional explanations do not take us very far. The most obvious possibility is that the proliferation of low-paying jobs is due mainly to recent changes in the American economy, particularly its transformation during the past generation from an industrial to a service economy. According to this view, the emphasis in America has gone from the manufacture of televisions and automobiles, which paid good wages, to the selling of these products, increasingly imported from abroad, with the result that the newly created jobs became disproportionately less productive and low-paying ones in the service sector. The Lamberts, the Bartelles, and Sandra Bolton have all held service sector jobs for their entire employment histories, except for the one year that Paul Lambert worked for Andrews' Electronics.

At the end of the 1950s, 31 percent of the nation's workers were employed in manufacturing industries, producing automobiles, steel, machine tools, and other items. Even as late as 1973, 27 percent of our workers were employed in manufacturing. By 1987, only 18 percent were, and the nation's balance of trade in manufactured products had plummeted deep into the red (see table 11). Many observers said our manufacturing plants and machinery had become outdated, no longer able to compete successfully with foreign companies. Images of crumbling industries starved for investment led to the labeling of them as "rust belt" industries and of the region where most of them were located as "the rust belt." Closings of factories and layoffs became common, and displaced employees had little choice except to take jobs in the service sector of the economy. Not even tariff and quota controls can stem the tide, the columnist Andrew Glass wrote, "as long as workers in Bangladesh

Table 11
PERCENTAGE OF MANUFACTURING WORKERS ON
NONAGRICULTURAL PAYROLLS AND BALANCE OF WORLD
TRADE IN MANUFACTURING, UNITED STATES, SELECTED
YEARS, 1965–1987

	Manufacturing Workers (in percentages)	Balance of Trade in Manufacturing (in billions of dollars)
1966	30.0	+ 4.8
1970	27.3	+ 3.4
1975	23.8	+ 19.8
1980	22.4	+ 18.8
1985	19.7	− 101.2
1987	18.6	− 141.2 [a]

[a] Adjusted for twelve months, on the basis of eleven-month figures.
Sources: For trade, Council of Economic Advisers, *Economic Report of the President, 1988,* p. 368, table B-105, and *1986,* p. 370, table B-102; for manufacturing workers, ibid., *1988,* p. 296, table B-43.

produce for 13 cents an hour what workers in South Carolina produce for $9.13 an hour."[11] As a result, calls have multiplied to help workers in our manufacturing industries increase their level of productivity so that they can compete with foreign rivals. Some advocate a comprehensive policy of reindustrialization to revitalize the manufacturing sector, while others advocate capital-gains and other tax reductions intended to spur new investment in these industries.[12]

These theories and proposed solutions suggest that as manufacturing jobs have disappeared, growing percentages of workers have had to take jobs at very low pay levels. Yet, though this view sounds logical, the evidence is unclear that low-paying jobs have proliferated as manufacturing employment declined. Low-paying jobs in the American economy are nothing new. Such jobs typically abounded even when employment in manufacturing was near its peak. In 1973, the proportion of manufacturing jobs in the economy was fully 25 percent higher than it was in 1985. However, research that compares the earnings over time of all workers

Table 12

PERCENTAGE OF ALL AMERICAN WORKERS WITH LOW, MIDDLE, AND HIGH EARNINGS,*
1973–1985

| | Shares of Employment | | | | Net Changes in Shares in Employment | | |
Year	Low Earnings	Middle Earnings	High Earnings	Period	Low Earnings	Middle Earnings	High Earnings
1973	31.8	51.6	16.6	1973–1979	18.5	54.8	26.7
1979	30.1	52.0	17.9	1979–1985	21.6	54.6	23.9
1985	29.4	52.2	18.3				

* Low earnings equal less than 50 percent of median earnings in 1973, measured by the adjusted consumer price index; high earnings equal greater than 200 percent of median earnings in 1973.
Source: Marvin H. Kosters and Murray N. Ross, "A Shrinking Middle Class," *Public Interest*, no. 90 (Winter 1988): 25, table 5, line 4.

(whether full-time or not) has found that the proportion of American workers with low earnings did not change significantly during those years. The research defined low earnings as less than half the median earnings in 1973, adjusted for inflation to 1985. For a year-round full-time worker in 1985, these earnings paid about four-fifths the amount a family of three needed to attain self-sufficiency. The research found that workers with low earnings constituted more than 30 percent of all employees in 1973. This was actually slightly larger than the proportion of employees with low earnings in 1985 (see table 12). Moreover, low-paying employment represented only about 20 percent of the new jobs created during those years.

Other studies, focusing exclusively on year-round full-time jobs, have come to a different conclusion. They suggest that the incidence of low-paying jobs created after 1979 may be closer to 35 percent, not 20 percent.[13] However, even this research discovered that the overall proportion of fully employed American workers who held low-paying jobs in 1986 (17.2 percent) was smaller than the proportion found in 1963 (21.4 percent), although employment in American manufacturing and America's technological superiority in world trade were at their zenith in 1963.[14] As table 13 shows,

Table 13
RATIO OF AVERAGE EARNINGS OF THE TOP AND BOTTOM ONE-FIFTH OF
AMERICAN WORKERS TO THE MIDDLE FIFTH OF WORKERS, 1950–1986, BY
GENDER

	Male Earners		Female Earners	
	Top One-fifth	Bottom One-fifth	Top One-fifth	Bottom One-fifth
1950	183.5	18.3	234.7	10.5
1960	195.1	13.2	280.7	11.6
1970	204.7	12.6	272.6	10.1
1980	223.0	14.4	247.8	12.3
1986	241.0	14.3	268.0	12.3

Source: Gary Burtless, "Earnings Inequalities over the Business Cycles," in Gary
Burtless, ed., *A Future of Lousy Jobs: The Changing Structure of U.S. Wages* (Washington, D.C.: Brookings Institution, 1990), p. 116, table A-1.

too, the earnings of the worst-paid (the lowest one-fifth) of
the American workers relative to the average American
worker does not appear to have changed much since 1960,
notwithstanding the dramatic reduction of the percentage of
our workers in manufacturing jobs. The bottom did not fall
out from underneath the worst-paid jobs as compared with
the average job. The gap has even narrowed a little since
1970. Although a widening of the inequality in earnings did
occur, it was confined to a rise in earnings of male workers
in the top fifth of earners; it did not involve a loss of earnings by workers in the bottom fifth relative to the average.
To the extent that the gap between low-earning workers and
average workers is considered excessive, it appears to be a
long-term condition rather than a recent one.

On the other hand, the average American worker has not
done very well for quite some time now, and American
manufacturing has certainly made a contribution here. The
average wage among manufacturing workers has failed to
increase in real terms for more than a decade. Indeed, manufacturing workers may themselves have difficulty getting
above the threshold of self-sufficiency. Machine operators

Table 14
PERCENTAGE OF FULLY EMPLOYED MANUFACTURING WORKERS LIVING IN HOUSEHOLDS BENEATH
ECONOMIC SELF-SUFFICIENCY, IN 1989

	Production Supervisors	Metal-workers	Other Precision Products	Machine Operators	Assemblers	Production Inspectors	All Manu-facturing Production Workers
Percentage of All Fully Employed Workers Living in Households beneath Economic Self-sufficiency	2.3	6.2	9.4	12.4	11.2	6.9	9.3
Percentage of Fully Employed Workers with a High School Degree Living in Households beneath Economic Self-sufficiency	1.5	5.1	6.4	9.7	7.6	6.6	7.6

Source: Figures are compiled from the Current Population Survey tapes.

compose the largest group of manufacturing workers, for example. More than 12 percent of these workers had incomes beneath self-sufficiency in 1989, though they worked full-time for the entire year (see table 14). The same is true for 9.7 percent of the machine operators with high school degrees.

We have been told that the compensation of American manufacturing workers turned sluggish following the early 1970s because the industries of rival nations, such as West Germany, had advanced more quickly in technological prowess, leading to greater productivity increases (higher output per hour of labor). This enabled their industries to compete more effectively in ever-toughening global markets. Leaders who advocate investment incentives through capital-gains-tax reductions or propose reindustrialization policies claim that additional or better-placed investment to improve industrial productivity is a key to strengthening the competitiveness of American industries and, with it, the level

Table 15

PRODUCTIVITY INCREASES AND REAL COMPENSATION PER
HOUR OF MANUFACTURING WORKERS IN THE UNITED STATES
AND WEST GERMANY, 1978–1988
(PERCENTAGE CHANGE)

	Productivity	Real Hourly Compensation*
United States	+34.2	−1.5
West Germany	+31.8	+28.9

*In national currency adjusted by the rise in consumer prices from
1978 to 1988 in each country. Compensation includes both pay and
benefits.
Source: U.S. Department of Labor, *Handbook of Labor Statistics,
1989,* p. 561, table 146, and p. 576, table 151.

of wages of American workers. Raising worker productivity
is a sure path to better-paying jobs, they say.

However, from 1978 to 1988,[15] the productivity of
America's manufacturing workers improved by an impres-
sive 34 percent (see table 15). That is, manufacturing workers produced 35 percent more output for each hour worked
in 1988 than they had ten years earlier. Nevertheless, the
compensation that they received did not increase. Table 15
shows that by 1988 the real compensation of our manufacturing workers per hour had actually declined 1 percent, on
the average, since 1978, notwithstanding the 34 percent
advance in the productivity of workers. By contrast, West
Germany's manufacturing workers improved their productivity by 32 percent during the same ten years, slightly less
than the improvement that American workers registered.
Nevertheless, the average real compensation of the German
workers per hour grew by 29 percent, or 30 percent more
than the real compensation of America's workers.[16]

We cannot ascribe this discrepancy to the possibility that
American manufacturing workers had been paid excessively
compared with West German workers prior to 1978 and
that German workers were only catching up during the subsequent years. West Germany's manufacturing workers had

equaled the hourly compensation of their American counterparts as early as 1975; by 1979, their hourly compensation surpassed that of America's manufacturing workers.[17] Nor does it appear that West Germany had an absolute lead in productivity that enabled its compensation to advance more rapidly than America's. The German advantage in compensation appears to have occurred even though America's manufacturing workers perform with higher absolute productivity than do West Germany's.[18]

Poor management of American companies in the areas of marketing and sales, ineffective national economic policies, faulty governmental foreign exchange policies,[19] comparatively large resources given to management pay and financial manipulations in American companies, and a number of other factors[20] might help explain the substantial discrepancy in the wage increases of American and West German workers compared with their relative gains in productivity. No one can be certain of the explanation at this juncture. No explanation, in any case, could deny that substantial productivity improvements of millions of American workers during an entire decade did not translate into any real increases in compensation for the workers, let alone ones commensurate with the size of the productivity improvements or with the advances in compensation enjoyed by workers in some other countries.

POLICY IMPLICATIONS

From start to finish, conventional explanations for low wages and working poverty fall short of providing adequate answers. Although some answers focus on poor education or discrimination, working poverty in America reaches well beyond high school dropouts, or the educationally low-skilled, or single parents, or minorities and women. Obstacles faced by these groups do influence earnings, but they do not explain why large numbers of white males with high school degrees or some college training also find themselves in working poverty, including even quite a few who have educational skills above the national average. The transformation of America's economy away from an industrial base and the loss of manufacturing jobs does not appear to have been a decisive influence, either. Even the supposedly slow productivity growth of the nation's manufacturing industries that allegedly undermined its global competitiveness and thus the wages of industrial workers at home leaves much evidence unexplained.

Nonetheless, despite their limitations, these and other explanations provide the foundation for many of the leading proposals attempting to attack the problem of economic hardship. Some proposals, such as those that would deny driver's licenses or public welfare to school dropouts, aim to alleviate working poverty by supporting programs that encourage teenagers to finish high school. Other proposals, such as federal aid to education, allowing parental choice of their children's schools, national testing, and the development of model schools, strive to improve the quality of the schools and educational systems across the nation so as to increase the competency and skills of graduating students. Proposals that would focus on completion of high school and improvement of education as solutions to working poverty miss a crucial point. Completing high school *is* important, but this solution ignores that many fully employed high school graduates end up with incomes beneath self-sufficiency. They indeed do so at the same rate as the entire full-time working population. Workers who have completed some college education and have academic skills above the national median fare only moderately better. Even they are vulnerable.

Other proposals call for stronger equal opportunity and affirmative action programs. Advocates here fail to take into account that although gender and race do lead to differential pay—a problem that should be addressed—they do not contribute significantly to working poverty. Fully employed white males are only slightly less likely to be in working poverty than the full-time working population as a whole.

Still other proposals call for reindustrialization. These proposals fail to answer findings of long-term studies that disclose only a moderate relationship between the proportion of Americans working in manufacturing jobs and the proportion of American workers in low-paid jobs. Proposals aimed at lifting the nation's manufacturing productivity by upgrading the skills of workers or by reducing taxes in order to spur investment in industry fail to mention that, unlike those in other countries, productivity improvements by manufacturing workers in America between 1978 and 1988 did not lead, on the average, to any real compensation increases for the workers.

All of these proposals have merit; successful implementation of them would possibly help restrain increases in working poverty and promote advances in productivity, and they could also improve pay equity for groups now receiving disproportionately low pay. No argument is made here to ignore these strategies. But present knowledge yields little confidence that they can or will provide an effective antidote to working poverty.

Not even economic expansion appears to be a compelling solution. Historically, policymakers and the public in America have hoped that the economy's dynamism will enlarge the employment and wage opportunities available to American workers. The economy has been dynamic. It has more than doubled in real size since the early 1960s, and generated 45 million new jobs, a 65 percent increase.[21] Moreover, during that time, the overall efficiency (productivity) of the work force has risen by about 50 percent.[22] Despite the economy's rapid growth, eighteen million Americans remain in the families of fully employed workers who live beneath self-sufficiency. Even since 1973, the economy has expanded by 50 percent in real terms. That is, the economy is now half again as large in real terms as it was in 1973. It has created 33 million new jobs. Although the productivity advance per worker hour slowed following 1973, it still improved by nearly 20 percent,[23] and more so in manufacturing, as we have seen. Yet, since 1973, the average hourly real wage of America's production workers has not risen; instead, it has declined by more than 10 percent—30 percent below the advance in productivity over those years.[24]

A shortage of decent-paying jobs exists in the American economy—that much we know—yet the shortfall seems to defy adequate explanation.[25] In the end, the root problem of the scarcity of jobs paying decent wages may have no exact cause or set of causes that we can delineate and validate, let alone figure out how to solve very effectively. All the same, a lack of knowledge of decisive causes of the job shortage does not negate the reality. Contrary to the American ethos, millions of American families live in a world of economic distress even though they contain fully employed workers. To change the circumstances that hardworking Americans face will require an awareness of our lack of understanding of the precise causes behind the shortage of decent-paying jobs and a recognition that today's commonly proposed cures for working poverty are inadequate. We need to begin the search for new solutions.

C h a p t e r   S i x

OTHER CASUALTIES OF
THE JOB SHORTAGE

The effect of the job shortage on American lives does not stop at fully employed workers who live beneath self-sufficiency. Although perhaps the most clear-cut, they are by no means the sole casualties. The fate of many impoverished workers who are not fully employed is inexorably tied to the economic conditions that face the fully employed poor. Because of the shortage of decent-paying jobs, workers may have little choice but to become employed intermittently or part-time, earning incomes beneath self-sufficiency because they cannot find steady full-time work at adequate wages. Like the fully employed, these Americans cannot provide decently for their families by practicing the work ethic. As many as six million more employed workers fall into this category beyond the fully employed who live beneath self-sufficiency.

One of the fiercest debates of American social policy during the past several decades, and indeed throughout American history, is about whether poor Americans who do not work full-time fail to do so because they cannot make ends meet through employment or because they are unmotivated and prefer to live on welfare. As far back as the 1820s, official reports for the states of New York and Massachusetts observed that the welfare system of that time (called poor relief) operated "as so many invitations to become beggars" and that the laws "frequently invite the able bodied vagrant to partake of the [relief] bounty."[1] The language now seems dated, but these statements contain a sentiment that is familiar today. During the 1980s, the belief that poor Americans were unwilling to work and could lift themselves out of their economic privation if they chose to take and keep full-time jobs became the clarion call of political leaders like Ronald Reagan as well as conservative scholars like Charles Murray and Lawrence Mead,[2] and a sizable segment of the public at large. The presumption here is that nearly all who wanted to work could find a job that would enable them to rise out of poverty. This being presumed, the debate about poverty increasingly came to focus on the large number of welfare recipients who did not work, leading to the many workfare experiments during the 1980s and ultimately the workfare reform of 1988. The way to attack poverty among the employable on welfare seemed clear: require them to work or to train for work. Otherwise, in President Reagan's words, they would remain no more than "a faceless mass waiting for handouts."[3]

Nonetheless, the scarcity of full-time employment at wages enabling workers to afford basic necessities does affect how workers behave. Even during the 1980s there were not enough jobs, not even at the minimum wage, to go around. A conservative estimate, by Lawrence Mead, suggests that there was an absolute deficit of jobs, including those at the minimum wage, for about 2.6 million job seekers in 1989.[4] Yet the minimum wage itself may be too low a standard to use in assessing the job deficit, since a single individual working at that wage could not reach self-sufficiency for a household of one, or even come close to it. The wage a fully employed worker needed in order to attain self-sufficiency for a single individual in 1989 was $4.90 an hour, about 30 percent higher than the minimum wage. Remember, the economy budget that measures self-sufficiency is a Spartan one. It makes no provision for many of the kinds of expenditures that Americans often take for granted and contains no money for emergencies. It seems understandable that jobs offering a fully employed worker discernibly less than the wage enabling a single individual to reach self-sufficiency (some of the jobs not assuring even continuous full-time work) might stay unfilled as workers kept looking for employment able to sustain them. This is not to speak of workers heading families containing children, who have still greater wage needs. In 1989, as we noted in chapter 5, eleven million year-round full-time jobs paid less than three-quarters of the income necessary to reach self-sufficiency for a family of three.

Although normally a minority opinion, the view that earnings from employment may leave large numbers of workers in poverty even during favorable economic times has a respectable following in America. Some of its fervent supporters come from the most surprising quarters, including people like Horatio Alger, the embodiment of the American ethos. His novels tell this very story. In Alger's fiction, hard work, diligence, and ambition invariably lead to success. Yet, while there is always a happy ending, the rags-to-riches ascent of Alger's characters never results mainly from the private economy's reward for ambition and hard work. Rather, a rich benefactor normally appears in the deserving character's life, outside any economic relationship, to reward the character with a gift of money or a good job for having done some brave deed. The gift, in turn, enables the ambitious and the honest to lift themselves above the others.

Alger's stories express faith in human virtues, but not in a free-market economy; such an economy was bound to glorify selfish action at the expense of humaneness and decency.

His stories frequently depict the plight of workers who "suffer from competition," and show how cut-throat competition, the natural outgrowth of selfish action, often produces starvation wages and ruin. Whereas others praised the free market, Alger criticized it. His *Bound to Rise* describes the grim plight of workers in the shoe trade: "It isn't steady. When it's good, everybody rushes into it, and the market soon gets overstocked. Then there's no work for weeks."[5] As a result of the mayhem of the free market and the disadvantageous position of workers relative to owners, Alger wrote in *Phil the Fiddler,* it is easy to find "the essential injustice of [workers] laboring without proper compensation."[6] This same theme about the payment of "low," "starvation," and "unrespectable" wages to workers appears in more than three dozen of his stories. Because the free market acts to depress wages for those at the bottom, reward and eventual success come, in his books, not from workers diligently taking up employment in an economy of low-paying jobs but from outside assistance given to the deserving—the ambitious and the honest—by benevolent rich men who occupy privileged positions. Virtually all of Alger's rags-to-riches stories follow this pattern.

THE STORY OF RAY AND BETH CLARK

In the winter of 1986, Ray Clark would have given anything for a wealthy benefactor to enter his life. This never happened. At the time, he had been unemployed and doing odd jobs for five months, unable to find work that would sustain his family.

Now thirty-five, Ray and his wife, Beth, thirty, have three young children. Their home is a two-room wooden house in a Florida farming community near the Gulf coast. The entire house, which they rent, is no larger than some living rooms. Beds for the three children crowd one of the rooms. The front door opens into the other room. A toilworn couch that doubles as a bed and an old stove sitting next to the wall opposite the front door occupy much of that room. The windows have new curtains with a flower design that brightens the room. The walls are bare except for children's art and a dish cabinet that hangs above the stove. The Clarks have lived here for five years, although Ray has been gone most of that time. Nearly four years ago, he was sent to prison.

Until late 1985, Ray was in the Air Force. He had joined when he was twenty-one, three years after getting his high school diploma in Pennsylvania. He was thinking of staying in the service for several years. Beth, who had grown up in Texas, went into the Air Force when she was nineteen, a year after high school. She met Ray during her first month in the service, and they got married one month later. They were in Colorado. "It was love at first sight," she said. "It has been ever since." She left the Air Force four years later, after her second child was born. Ray, who had become a staff sergeant, served another three years. Having moved three times during their marriage, Ray left the service hoping that the family could establish roots and that he could make a better living.

By late 1985, the country was in the midst of a prolonged period of economic growth. Beth and Ray had high hopes. Jobs were hard to get, however, harder than they had anticipated. It took Ray about six weeks to find a job as a landscape repairman and construction worker at six dollars an hour, employed forty to fifty hours a week, sometimes more. The job was exhausting. He would leave at about five in the morning and on some days get home at five or six in the evening. He was out all day digging, repairing machinery, and working pumps. The sun had turned his short red hair nearly blond and his otherwise pale skin into a leathery dark tan, etching indelible wrinkles by his eyes, Beth recalled. The outdoor work had put additional muscle on his six-foot frame.

As we sat in Beth's room talking about her life with Ray, we were interrupted several times by her youngest son, Jake, who was four years old. Even before Ray went to prison, Beth had stayed home caring for the three children, two of whom were not yet in school. She also earned a little money doing yard work and baby-sitting. Normally a placid person, Beth changed her demeanor around Jake. She became lighthearted and playful. She helped him discover new ways to play games with a bottle, a piece of cloth, or other items found around the house. Several times she stopped to read to him. As she did, she would add humorous embellishments to the stories, much to her and Jake's delight.

Beth vividly remembered the nearly sixteen-month period following Ray's separation from the service until he was sent to prison. Ray was employed full-time for approximately the first year of that period, and together Beth and he earned slightly less than $16,500. This income enabled them to rent the two-room house and maintain one car, a 1973 Oldsmobile that had traveled more than 150,000 miles. They had no health insurance.

"We had enough money for food," Beth said. "But it was lean. We definitely had to be very careful about how we spent our money. We were usually a month behind in paying bills, sometimes two. Electricity gets it one month, gas would get it the next month. We could never put the money together for new tires for our car, so we would get tires for ten to fifteen dollars and put them on. They'd last a couple of months, and then we'd have to do it again. It was really tight. We could count on my parents and brothers and sisters helping out in terms of things for the kids, clothes and things. Also [they] got us parts for car repairs since my brother owns a car repair shop, and my parents would give us maybe forty or fifty dollars a month."

"It was really frustrating," Beth continued. "He [Ray] really didn't want me to take regular work until Jake [who was then less than one] was old enough to be on his own a little more. He was working as hard as he could and couldn't have taken a second job. It wasn't practical. By the time he got home, he was spent. Nerves were on end. It was really tense, a small house, and it seemed like we were never able to really budget or save anything. Just living day to day. It wasn't really right. We definitely weren't going to get anywhere, any better than we had."

In August 1986, things took a decisive turn for the worse. Ray's boss called him in and said he had lost some contracts and could no longer afford Ray. It was a complete surprise. He gave Ray one week's notice.

"Ray got home about five o'clock that evening," Beth said. "He came in and looked a little more remorseful than usual, and exhausted and down. He said, 'I got fired today.' He was really down. I said, 'Why?' He said, 'It's hard to say.' He felt slapped down. He was sunburned and dirty, and he had a distant look in his eyes. He didn't say a whole lot. I was scared. We were kind of silent."

It was a Friday. The next Monday, Ray went to the unemployment office and got applications from landscape and construction companies. He applied for apartment maintenance work and for jobs fixing heating units and air conditioners. "He spent a lot of time looking for jobs," Beth said. "Every day he was out most of the day, and his boss also looked for him. He got some offers, too, but they were all giving four or four-fifty an hour [five to six dollars in 1991 dollars], this was all he could find. It's not feasible to support a family on that pay. There's no way you can keep up a family, no way to make it. We were earning a lot more than that on the landscaping job and weren't able to make it.

"He kept looking, and he did odd jobs when he could, a

lot of things—painting, yard work, fixing an air conditioner—and pulled in about $100 a week, plus $135 from unemployment, and I worked some. We also got some food stamps."

Four months later, Ray was still searching, every day when he wasn't on a job, still not finding anything beyond $4.50 an hour. Working at that pay with another part-time job on the side would leave him beneath even the official poverty line in 1986. Yet he could not make it on unemployment and doing odd jobs, either.

"By December, he said that we were broke and had bills to pay that we couldn't, and there's no Christmas for the kids," Beth recalled. "We had already given up the phone. It turned into a luxury. It wasn't a necessity, and [yet] it was. You don't really need it except as far as getting employment and people being able to contact you. But we didn't have the money.

"I think he felt there was no way out. He was more frustrated, apprehensive, and feeling he had failed us. And unemployment was going to run out. One evening he came over to me. He was real quiet, and he says, 'Beth, I'm going to go over to the coast and pick up a little pot and bring it up here.' He said, 'You know, it's $3,000 for one night. It'll pay for us for a while. We can make the payments on everything.' I told him I didn't want him to do it, that I didn't think it was a really good idea. I said the money was really tempting, and that you do what you feel you have to do, and if this is what you're really going to do, go ahead and do it, but it's not a good idea and I have a really bad feeling about it. 'I'm going to do it,' he said. 'We'll be all right. We'll be back in the morning.' Part of me felt it would be really nice to have $3,000. It would have really helped. It would have made a big difference."

Ray did not make it home that next morning. The police caught and arrested him on the highway a few miles from the coast. Beth said that she trembled upon hearing the news. He was tried, found guilty, and sentenced to a federal prison in another state.

"It's been four years of our lives," Beth said. "Long years." During that time she has lived on welfare and food stamps in addition to the money she earns from doing yard work, housecleaning, and baby-sitting. Her parents and several neighbors have also helped out. Considering child care and other costs she would incur with employment, she's been unable to find work that would pay much more than the jobs she is now doing around the neighborhood. It's hard to make it from day to day, she says. She runs out of money for food well before the month ends. Desperate though it is, however, it is not her economic situation but her longing for Ray that has been most devastating. The loneliness absorbs her "every day," she says. "The kids have taken it well, though. Rick and Jeanne [the two older children, aged ten and eight] miss him, but I don't see other effects. They cry, but they don't act up. I show them pictures, and we talk about him most days, and we get letters from him, and I assure them that he'll be back." Beth feared that Ray would be in continual danger in prison. However, he has not experienced violence, and this has calmed Beth's apprehensions.

Ray's term will be up in a few months. Beth said that, after his release, the family planned to move to Pennsylvania, near Ray's parents, and to start their lives again. She is optimistic. All three of the children will be in school, Beth said, and that will enable her to get a full-time job. She was concerned about the scars that Ray's term in prison might leave in him and the difficulties he will confront finding a new job. However, when she talked of Ray's imminent release and their upcoming move to Pennsylvania, her face brightened. For Beth, whose nature is to focus on the positive, the unknown future seems full of promise. The nightmare that tormented Ray and her in the past, she hopes, has finally come to an end.

JOB SCARCITY AND THE WORK FORCE AT LARGE

During 1986, that dismal and fateful year for the Clark family, Ray Clark felt isolated in his search for full-time work to sustain his family. He had lots of company, though. In 1986, many people like Ray Clark were employed part-time or for only part of the year because they were unable to get adequate full-year full-time employment. According to a study of income and employment records,[7] 3.4 million American households in 1986 were headed by males who had incomes beneath the official poverty line. Slightly more than 1 million of these males were retired or were ill or disabled. Of the remaining 2.3 million households, the heads of 984,000 (41.9 percent) *were* employed the whole year in 1986. The heads of another 741,000 households (31.5 percent) were employed for part of the year, reporting that they wanted to work the full year but were unable to find adequate work.[8] For every male employed the entire year living in a household beneath the official poverty line, there was thus nearly one part-year worker living beneath the poverty line who said he was unable to find adequate full-year work.

A large number of single-parent heads of households said the same. In 1986, some 386,000 single female heads of households living beneath the official poverty line who were employed for part of the year reported that the chief reason they were not working the whole year was their inability to find satisfactory full-year employment. This, once more, nearly equals the number (468,000) of single female heads of households in 1986 who were beneath the official poverty line who did hold full-year jobs.[9]

All these families lived beneath the official poverty line. Let us now turn to 1989 and early 1990 and consider workers with incomes beneath the threshold of self-sufficiency. In March of 1990, the Current Population Survey found that 11.5 million workers living beneath self-sufficiency in 1989 either were full-time employees when the survey was taken or reported that they were employed part-time or part-year because they were unable to find adequate full-time work.[10] This number came to 5.5 million workers beyond the nearly 6 million fully employed workers living beneath the line of self-sufficiency in 1989. The 5.5 million workers held full-time jobs that had not lasted for the entire prior year (in 1989, 3 million who became unemployed had been "job losers" as opposed to "job leavers," "new entrants," or "reentrants"); or they held jobs that were not full-time despite their desire to work full-time. About 29 million Americans lived in the families of these 11.5 million workers, all of whom were employed. In addition, 6.5 million workers were then unemployed, altogether without a job, and more still were discouraged workers who had dropped out of the labor force entirely. Usual estimates suggest that these numbered as many as 1 million.

To reach self-sufficiency, workers must overcome two problems. One is to find wages that can sustain their families. The plight of the year-round full-time workers living beneath self-sufficiency attests to this problem. The second problem is to find steady full-time employment. This means jobs that are actually full-time, that make up for slack periods, and that are full-year—jobs that do not disappear as businesses reorganize or go bankrupt. In early 1990, 11.5 million employed workers who lived beneath the threshold of self-sufficiency during the preceding year faced one or both of these two problems.

POLICY IMPLICATIONS FOR WELFARE REFORM

When a shortage of steady, decent-paying jobs exists on this scale, governmental programs that aim to enable people to become self-supporting will have difficulty succeeding. Nowhere has this truth been more evident than in the results of governmental and even private-foundation experimental programs to address the problems of welfare. These programs combine skills training, job counseling, and work experience in an effort to enable welfare recipients to get and keep jobs allowing them to become as self-supporting as possible. Key elements of the most recent federal welfare reform, the Family Support Act of 1988, were based on such programs.

The experimental programs have achieved moderate success in raising rates of employment and earnings among welfare recipients. San Diego's Saturation Work Initiative Model (SWIM) was one of the most successful of the government's experimental programs.[11] Upon entering the program, participants joined a two-week job search workshop operated by SWIM. Those without jobs after the workshop were assigned to unpaid work experience lasting three months. They also continued to participate in a biweekly job search program. After three months, if individuals remained unemployed, SWIM assessed and referred them to education and job-training programs. Individuals who failed to comply with the requirements of the program could have their welfare grants suspended, reduced, or terminated altogether.[12]

An evaluation of the SWIM program found that in its second year (1987) the program had resulted in an increase in employment of 9.4 percent (49.4 percent of the SWIM participants became employed, compared with 40 percent of a control group of welfare recipients, who had not been in the program).[13] The average earnings of the SWIM participants for the year ($2,903) were $657 greater than those of the control group ($2,246).[14] This earnings increase permitted a modest reduction in the amount of welfare assistance given to the SWIM participants, a development worth noting. However, the achievement of this increase in participants' average annual earnings to $2,903 pales when placed next to the income needed in 1987 to lift a family of two above even the official poverty line ($7,641), let alone the threshold of self-sufficiency ($11,843).

Experimental programs of private foundations have not fared much better. One of the most successful of these experiments is the San Jose Center for Employment Training Program, sponsored by the Rockefeller Foundation. It could outperform the governmental programs, its sponsors believed, because it integrated basic education (reading and math skills) into the job-training program as these skills were pertinent to a specific job.[15] Again unlike the typical federal program, the job-training program in San Jose also simulated actual workplace conditions. It increased employment by 10 percent (46 percent for the participants, compared with 36 percent for a control group).[16] This was similar to the SWIM results. The average annual earnings of all the San Jose participants ($4,992) were 47 percent higher than those of the control group ($3,396).[17] This marks a considerable success. Nevertheless, even this success left the San Jose participants' incomes, on the average, well beneath the official poverty line, with the result that the public assistance the participants received ($291 a month) was only marginally lower than the assistance the control group received ($306 a month).[18]

It is perhaps noteworthy that the San Jose program, the most effective of the four experimental programs the Rockefeller Foundation attempted, also started with the lowest proportion of high school graduates, 32 percent.[19] Participants who had not completed high school might have the most to gain from the integrated education and training program. The other three programs, which had virtually no impact on either employment or earnings, to judge by the control groups,[20] contained not only higher percentages of participants who started with at least a high school degree (between 43 and 56 percent) but also more than 10 percent who had some college education.[21] About half the SWIM participants, too, were high school graduates.[22]

The federal Family Support Act of 1988 is unlikely to be able to do much better than the most successful experiments in bringing about self-sufficiency through employment for welfare recipients. A year before Congress passed the act, the Congressional Budget Office estimated the probable impact of a similar workfare program. It estimated that the workfare program would enable fewer than 10 percent of the participants to leave the welfare rolls during the first five years of its operation.[23] This level of effectiveness, if obtained, is worth the effort. All the same, even if obtained, it would leave more than 90 percent of the participants unaffected with respect to welfare and surely leave still more of them beneath the line of self-sufficiency.[24]

A private-market approach has proved highly effective, although the conditions for its success suggest the size of the problem the nation faces and the inherent limitations of the approach. Private companies, now operating in cities such as New York and Los Angeles, contract with state or city governments to train and then obtain jobs for welfare recipients. An example is America Works.[25] The government pays for its service only when welfare recipients have accepted and continued on a job for a prescribed period of time. The jobs are usually decent-paying ones, generally starting at $14,000. The cost to the government ($5,000 in the case of New York City's contract with America Works) is four times greater than the costs typically associated with governmental job-training and counseling programs. The San Diego SWIM program, for example, cost about $1,200 for each participant. However, the larger cost would earn a quick return if the program enabled participants to leave the welfare rolls permanently, which is likely to occur if participants obtain decent-paying jobs. A more substantial limitation of the approach is that the result can apparently be achieved for only a few people at a time, if only because of the limited number of available jobs. A typical contract involving America Works, for example, stipulates that the company will take a maximum of 200 clients. In 1988, the first year America Works contracted with New York, the state of New York had more than 300,000 adults on welfare.[26]

The record tells us that forms of workfare—whether run by the government, private foundations, or private enterprise—will not enable most low-income Americans to attain self-sufficiency. No matter how much we wish it otherwise, workfare cannot be an effective solution. Among the most important reasons for this is the absence of enough steady, decent-paying, full-time jobs to go around. Nearly twelve million employed workers are affected by this job shortage, unable to afford basic necessities while practicing the work ethic. It should be no surprise, then, that workfare participants, including those who found employment, have also been caught in this vise. In their inability to attain self-sufficiency, the employed participants of the workfare programs have reflected the experience of millions of other American workers from all backgrounds, many of them fully employed and academically skilled, who have been unable to attain self-sufficiency.

The nation's public policies, including workfare, can provide the key that these twelve million workers and their families need, along with recipients of welfare, to enable them to unlock the door to self-sufficiency. But the policies can do so only if they couple their present emphasis on getting people to seek and take jobs with a new focus on overcoming the dearth of steady, decent-paying jobs in America.

C h a p t e r   S e v e n

A VIEW FROM
CITY HALL*

Over the past decade, the federal government has increasingly turned to state and local governments for help in solving the problems facing the nation. The administrations of both President Reagan and President Bush have fought to reinvigorate federalism, arguing that state and local governments are closest to problems, and understand them better, and that there is greater room for creativity and experimentation at the state and local level. State and local actions to generate economic development run at a feverish pace. These governments spend much time and energy trying to improve their economies so as to create more and better jobs. Before looking to a national solution, we should ask whether the states and localities have discovered strategies to generate economic development in a manner that will make a decisive difference in the lives of the working poor.

At the national level, the conflicts over economic policy

* The principal author of this chapter is Thomas J. Volgy, mayor of the city of Tucson, Arizona, from 1987 to 1991.

1 0 7

often occur in sterile, abstract, economic terms: unemployment, inflation, recession. At the local level, the conflicts take on a human face.

As mayor of my city, I have seen the human faces. I would receive calls from constituents angry about their three-month battles to find jobs that will allow them to pay rent and utilities. I would hear from the owner of a restaurant demanding to know what city hall will do about the dearth of patrons who can afford to go out to dinner, threatening his future and that of his suppliers. Or I would look out my window and see three hundred merchants march on city hall, demanding to know what the city will do about their high bankruptcy rates. They wanted their taxes and fees eliminated, and they wanted regulations, which seemed to cause them little difficulty before now, to be relaxed. And it was no easier, having worked for sixteen months to attract one employer with eighteen hundred new jobs to the community, to read newspaper editorials denouncing the low wages these jobs will bring in the service industry.

At the National League of Cities and at the U.S. Conference of Mayors, during the breaks from committee meetings and plenary sessions, we would speak in subdued tones about the anguish brought by our economic struggles. I would nod in recognition as my colleagues talked about how painful it was to hear from a weeping mother wanting someone to tell her how her family will survive for six months on the "waiting list" for public housing. The same has happened to me: she and her husband both work for the minimum wage, and they lost their home to the mortgage company. My colleagues knew what I had to tell her: there were eleven hundred families on the waiting list in front of her.

Economic development problems at the local level can seem overwhelming. The problem is not only to create new jobs but to maintain existing jobs as well. It is a struggle not only to generate an infusion of jobs from the outside but also to promote the viability and expansion of existing businesses within the community. The challenge in the end is to create decent-paying jobs, ones that will sustain families and provide the kind of opportunities that are simply not available at minimal or low wages.

While the debate in Congress centers on industrial policy, tariffs, enterprise zones, and capital-gains cuts, the battle at the local level is over jobs and wages, and takes place simultaneously on several fronts. There is intense competition with other cities over a limited number of employers who may wish to relocate. Constant battles are fought with the federal government over the declining interest in, and resources for, urban problems. Battles are fought with multinational corporations that consider leaving our cities when economic advantages crop up in Mexico or other Third World locales. Those local interests that seek precious community resources in order to attract outside industry also battle small businesses within the community trying to use the same resources.

The story of how the battle is fought by the city of Tucson, in itself, is of little importance except perhaps to Tucsonans. But the trials and tribulations of this city mirror those of most municipalities around the nation. Although each city is unique in some respects, and consequently the specific development plan may change from city to city, the broad strategies we used in Tucson to achieve a stronger economy are the same as those in other cities. Our experience illustrates all too well the difficulties and dilemmas most states and municipalities face as they work to make life better for their communities. The story of our city may not be one of failure. But like that of cities as disparate as Portland, Dallas/Fort Worth, Hartford, Columbus, Birmingham, and many others all around the nation, it is not a success story either. This is true particularly with respect to the plight of the working poor. The nation needs to understand why success is so elusive in order to recognize that initiative, creativity, and action at the state and local levels will not do much to remedy the problems facing most of the working poor.

PATHS TO ECONOMIC PROGRESS OR ROADS
TO NOWHERE?

Ever since I ran for the office of mayor of Tucson, Arizona, a city of 409,000, my dream had been to nurture our heritage while offering our citizens more choices and opportunities for the future. I learned from my time in office what scores of other mayors from large, medium-sized, and small cities already know: the opportunity for turning the dream into reality is consistently blocked by a persistent and gnawing problem facing all of us. Although we all see our own communities as unique and special, the problem confronting my community is no different from that of most communities across America—inadequate numbers of jobs and, as important, too few decent-paying jobs. The crisis of low wages threatens to choke the future of most cities and to destroy the quality of life in them. And so, my hopes, like those of many of my colleagues throughout the country, had narrowed. The nurturing of a grand vision gave way to the more specific task of the daily grind of searching for better-paying jobs for citizens in the community. When we compared notes at national and regional conferences, I found that I resembled most mayors in this respect. Like them, I expected, when I started in office, to devote perhaps a third of my time to economic development. But confronted daily with the misery of those who work hard and yet have no hope, and the reality of businesses that have difficulty surviving, let alone expanding, I ended up devoting nearly 70 percent of my time to fighting for new jobs and preserving the jobs that we have.

Most states and municipalities around the country are moving toward comprehensive and "mixed" economic development strategies.[1] Traditionally, the search for more and better jobs has been based on plans focusing on existing capital, with state and local governments supporting low-risk undertakings and competing aggressively with other jurisdictions for the same investments and companies. More recently, this approach has been blended with "demand side" policies, which promote the discovery or expansion of new markets for local goods and services, including the search for new capital to help new businesses to form and existing businesses to expand. The combination of these approaches is expected to lead to a healthy economic environment and the creation of additional better-paying jobs.

Our city has followed this road. In order to overcome the anarchy of economic development where every segment of the community formulated its own battle plan and spent its own, highly limited resources, we created an umbrella organization to formulate an overarching economic development strategy. Today, instead of seventeen separate public and private economic development organizations, which rarely coordinated their activities in the past, the public sector and the private sector pool their resources and efforts to address the problems of the economy.

Next, we created a common agenda. Like the plans of many other cities, ours contained an economic strategy that attempted to build on the special strengths of the community. For example, since we are given high marks for our quality of life, we set about to attract new headquarters operations by targeting businesses in those parts of the country where the quality of life is deteriorating. Relying on the strength of the University of Arizona and its research capabilities, we pursued as well the creation of new start-up firms locally, and we sought manufacturing firms from outside of the community whose focus was on new high-technology, information-intensive manufacturing operations. We even focused on creating economic advantage from the rich multicultural heritage of the community by expanding our international sister-city cultural programs and using them to promote overseas trade by our own businesses. We tried every reasonable strategy, including the expansion of job-training programs for the working poor, the streamlining of government services, and technological assistance and loan programs for small businesses.

No matter how hard they may try or how innovative they may be, local communities encounter two major problems with their economic strategies. One is the issue of finding the necessary resources to implement the battle plan. The other is that, even when implemented, all these activities combined may lead to little actual success in creating the kind of jobs needed by the working poor.

A diversified economic strategy cannot be implemented by simply formulating a blueprint for a healthy economy. A strategy designed to create jobs, economic stability, and higher wages is ultimately dependent upon finding ample resources with which to wage the battle. In our case, it has meant generating new resources in a number of realms. Public-sector resources for economic development were doubled at both the city and the county levels. Next, new funding mechanisms were established to generate private-sector contributions to match public resources. Most important, an aggressive strategy was developed to generate assistance from the state.

Like those of many other cities, however, our efforts were handicapped by the reality that federal programs to assist job creation shriveled in every category during the 1980s. The new resources the states and cities have tapped over the last decade pale next to the federal cutbacks. Economic Development Administration assistance programs fell by 66 percent. Urban Development Action grants were reduced by 35 percent. Small Business Administration programs declined by 64 percent. Community development bloc grant programs were cut by 10 percent. In these four categories alone, economic development assistance to cities, in real dollars, plummeted by more than 50 percent in less than a decade.[2]

Can the cities fashion a response to economic needs despite shrinking federal assistance? Tough choices have been necessary. A recent survey of municipalities found that 72 percent of the cities surveyed raised taxes, while 42 percent raised taxes and cut services.[3]

In desperation, cities have turned to their states to help with the effort to create better jobs and are now vying with one another on the steps of their state capital. However, the stark reality in many states is that state resources have already been committed, often for programs that will not directly affect economic development efforts. The average contribution from states to their municipalities over a decade of shrinking federal resources has increased very little, from 11.1 percent of municipal budgets in 1980 to 12.2 percent in 1990. Moreover, the states have no additional resources. Some states, such as Massachusetts and Michigan, have worked closely with their cities to assist in infrastructure improvements that would lead to new and better-paying jobs. However, as the 1990s began, these two states, along with two-thirds of all states in the nation, are reporting significant budget deficits, which will force major reductions in their own programs.[4]

The mayors of the nation's cities cannot increase their local contributions much beyond what has already been done. Another increase in taxes when people are struggling is not an available option. We can eliminate or reduce other governmental programs in search of additional economic development resources, but cutbacks in basic services will only harm people further and, not incidentally, damage our attractiveness to incoming industry.

The difficulties in local economies caused by low wages create something of a catch-22 situation for local government. Low wages and inadequate jobs mean low purchasing power for many citizens, and that in turn creates insufficient governmental tax revenues, especially for those cities that are heavily dependent on sales taxes. Resources for economic development cannot be increased without cutting into existing programs. Yet when the economy is hampered by low wages, people who live on the margins of self-sufficiency demand more services for emergency shelter and food, public transportation, transitional housing, police, and social programs. Meeting these basic needs means that fewer resources for economic development will be available, further compounding the suffering for citizens. Shifting resources to the economic realm in turn heightens suffering for citizens who are already experiencing great difficulty in making ends meet.

One way a community might try to strengthen its economy and to create jobs with higher wages is to develop its industrial base from the inside—to create new indigenous industries.[5] But the scarcity of resources is a vital consideration here. Generating a new industrial base—such as, in our case, developing companies based on biomedical technology—requires venture capital (not available in large amounts for most local jurisdictions), additional educational infrastructure (for example, the development of a good high school science and other training programs for future employees), and physical infrastructure improvements (for example, upgrading transportation networks and water supply and delivery systems). Even the "narrower" strategies involving, in our case, the encouragement of tourism and convention activity often require major infrastructure investments for new convention facilities, hotels, and airports. The provision of such infrastructure is extremely expensive for most cities. That makes it virtually impossible to carry out such projects in a comprehensive manner; even when narrowed in scope, they cut off the flow of resources to other economic development tasks.

These long-term strategies are also quite costly from a political perspective. While long-term investments in infrastructure improvements or in indigenous industry are wise ones, the economic payoffs are long-term; in the short term, the suffering from inadequate wages or insufficient employment will virtually guarantee a political backlash and an erosion of the political will for long-term solutions. As a consequence, few communities will be able to commit their resources exclusively to long-term solutions. The hunt for quicker fixes is also essential.

As a result, cities usually engage in modest investments coordinated with other, less expensive strategies. One increasingly popular strategy is to look to foreign nations for markets and capital. Foreign markets add to the demand for local goods and services, leading to direct benefits in business expansion and greater job creation for those who need better wages. Investments from overseas can assist municipalities as well by underwriting infrastructure improvements critical to the development of indigenous industry. No wonder, then, that, long before the Reagan and Bush administrations were championing free-trade agreements with Canada and Mexico, enterprising cities throughout the nation were actively pursuing trade arrangements with their sister cities on four continents. Today, mayors are as likely to meet in the airport lobbies of Frankfurt and Tokyo as in Washington, D.C. Three years ago, sixty-nine American mayors descended on their counterparts in Tashkent for an economic development conference. Portland's economic presence is found in Osaka, Fort Worth is active in Budapest, New Yorkers are seeking economic opportunity in Beijing, Japanese investors are dining with city officials in Phoenix, and Tucson has trade offices in Taiwan and Guadalajara.

Generating jobs through an active involvement in the global economy is serious business, but cities have also engaged in their fair share of fads while trying to improve conditions for workers with low wages. One of these is the concept of enterprise zones. Enterprise zones are created and superimposed typically on a geographical area within the community that is composed of low-income families. Government incentives, often in the form of tax inducements and job-training programs, are provided to businesses if they bring new jobs to the targeted area. In addition, programs as a rule require that a certain percentage of workers must be hired from the targeted area. Enterprise zones have been tried in a number of cities and states, as well as overseas. Great Britain has considerable experience with them,[6] and in the United States there are now no fewer than five hundred enterprise zones.[7] The results are not very encouraging. One problem with enterprise zones is that they may create incentives for businesses to move from one part of the community to another, without creating any additional net jobs. Similarly, businesses may move from one community to another in search of further incentives where enterprise zones exist, but this effort only pits cities against one another for the same jobs without much real additional job creation at the state or regional level.

Even if we ignore the problem of competition for a finite number of jobs, still another, larger problem arises with this strategy. While it is possible that enterprise zones can attract more jobs into the community from elsewhere or perhaps even stimulate more business start-ups internally, these zones are no more likely to provide higher wages for the community than any of the other strategies we have devised. One recent review of enterprise zones comes to the same, discouraging conclusion on the basis of the experience with these programs throughout the last decade: generally, the "state and local tax breaks are of only minimal importance in persuading businesses to set up shop in enterprise zones and . . . the incentives can't be credited with creating jobs." Similarly, when the Bush administration asked the General Accounting Office for an analysis of the value of enterprise zones in Maryland, the auditors reported that enterprise zones in that state "did not stimulate local economic growth as measured by employment or strongly influence most employers' decisions about business location."[8]

Enterprise zones may be a fad, and their consequences rather more apparent than real, but they do form a part of the larger array of tools being used by local governments in the search to attract new employers from other parts of the United States. In the 1990s, cities are involved in a deadly serious competition with one another to attract scarce new employment opportunities that often lead to more jobs (but not necessarily higher wages). In my city, virtually every new employer came under conditions of rigorous competition between our community and scores of other cities. In some cases, we literally won out over one hundred other cities for a single employer.

The steps are the same from one end of the nation to the other. Out of one hundred prospective employers being courted, a successful city will typically "win" no more than half a dozen businesses. In many cases, the prospective employer is in search of "incentives" to sweeten the bottom line. In return, jobs are promised. Sometimes, tax incentives, training incentives, or infrastructure improvements offered by local municipalities are tied both to a certain number of jobs provided by the prospective employer and to the length of time the prospective employer will have to remain in the community. In a few cases, the municipalities may also link such incentives to a wage rate "range," but such restrictions are rarely made, for fear of losing the potential employer altogether or of unduly interfering with the "market" for determining private-sector wages. In the vast majority of cases, little is known in advance of the wages coming in to the local community apart from vague commitments that the wages will be "competitive."

Once the decision is made, it is announced with great fanfare. Immediately following the announcement, calls and letters of congratulations arrive. But the euphoria is short-lived. Soon, citizens begin to call city hall, demanding to know why they are not being hired. Local businesses write letters to newspapers, demanding to know why they don't receive the same incentives provided to the newcomers. A number of social service organizations inquire why the city is not spending resources to secure higher paid wages than those being offered by the new company. Meanwhile the quest for new jobs continues.

Most cities are caught in a vicious trap; the search is for better-paying jobs. However, no job can be turned down, since lower-paying jobs are better than no jobs at all. Withholding resources from potential employers in the hope of attracting better-paying jobs with the same resources leads to longer-term unemployment for those who suffer from the lack of any jobs in the community.

Under the best of circumstances, the ability of local governments to alleviate the problems associated with low wages through economic development strategies is bound to have limited success. The experience of my community bears telling precisely because we implemented the full range of economic development strategies available to local governments and overcame numerous problems and yet, despite all this, were unable to significantly aid the working poor in our city.

We pursued the strategy of wooing companies into our community. At one level it paid off. Within twelve months following community agreement about our economic development strategy, we generated four thousand additional jobs for our city. We also lost a major employer, whose employees held two thousand good-paying manufacturing jobs, but our efforts overcame these losses and yielded significantly more jobs than had been available to the community previously. This rate of job creation had never been equaled in our history. I listened with great pride as spokespeople for the new companies publicly elaborated on the virtues of our community, the competitiveness of our economic development efforts, the strength of our labor force, and the fine quality of life their executives would enjoy in our city. Our unemployment level reached a new low, falling at one point to 3.1 percent. Our newspapers vied with one another and the electronic media for the newest "scoop" in reporting the latest economic breakthrough.

We were also successful in our quest for overseas trade and capital. One trade magazine placed us among the top ten cities in international trade.[9] Mayors of other cities spoke to me with envy about the companies that chose my city over theirs.

Additionally, we invested in our own capabilities. A variety of new businesses opened, manufacturing products in optics and biomedical technology. These businesses came about as spin-offs from the scientific research being conducted by the University of Arizona. The infusion of loans and venture capital strengthened existing businesses. Our local development agency poured millions of dollars in loans into small businesses and secured hundreds of new jobs as these businesses used the loans to expand their activities.

What types of jobs did we generate? The best we could find. A few, particularly in the aerospace industry, paid excellent wages. The vast remainder, whether in manufacturing or in services, often paid no more than $5.50 to $7.50 per hour. The wages created through the expansion of our development programs for indigenous small businesses paid about the same, although these companies' benefits packages were weaker than those offered by incoming firms.

We increased the numbers of jobs in our community, and our unemployment rate decreased, but the standard of living for our citizens has not increased. Despite the hard work, despite the "game plan," the rosy glow from another "victory" in generating new employment has not translated into meaningful choices of better-paying jobs for the working poor.

The experiences of my city are not very different from those of others around the nation, whether or not their governments have created comprehensive efforts to develop economic planning. Research has found that the variety of

Table 16

ECONOMIC DEVELOPMENT STRATEGIES, OVERALL JOB INCREASES, MANUFACTURING
JOB INCREASES, AND WAGE INCREASES FOR STATES, 1984–1989 (N = 48)
(IN PERCENTAGES)

Economic Development	Increase in All Jobs[a]	Increase in Manufac- turing Jobs[a]	Increase in Wages Manufac- turing Jobs	Increase in Wages All Jobs
Successful States[b]	17.2	7.3	19.0	18.4
Unsuccessful States	13.4	1.3	22.5	21.5

[a] The percentages of job increases reflect the aggregate average of the percentage increases of
the individual states in each category and as a result are slightly different from the increase in
jobs for the nation as a whole.

[b] Successful states are those that developed a statewide economic strategy in the early to mid-
1980s and generated additional jobs beyond the national average in total jobs, manufacturing jobs, or both.

Source: U.S. Department of Labor, Bureau of Labor Statistics, *Employment and Earnings:
Annual Averages,* vol. 32–37 (1985–90).

tools available to states and cities to spur economic development brings, at best, little more than a marginal rise in
local wage levels.[10] In fact, on the average, every such policy
a state enacts and implements benefits a family of four
approximately seventeen dollars a year in additional income,
an increase of about one two-thousandth.[11] A review of the
range of economic development strategies available to states
determined that of the thirty-eight strategies that states use,
only five are even meant to affect wages directly.[12]

No wonder, then, that states may be successful in generating jobs in general, and even manufacturing jobs, but such
successes do not necessarily translate into better wages and
may do little to improve economic conditions for the working poor. We examined the experiences of states over five
years during the 1980s and found that their economic development strategies led to little growth in the wages of workers. For example, eleven states in the nation implemented an
economic development strategy and pursued it "successfully" to the extent that they experienced new-job creation
above and beyond the national average. As table 16 shows,

"successful" states outperformed "unsuccessful" states both in the total numbers of jobs they created (nearly one-third more) and in terms of increases in manufacturing jobs (more than five times as many).

Yet, even with economic development programs and above-average job increases, the growth of wage levels in the "successful" states was slower than the growth of wages in the "unsuccessful" states. In fact, the wage increases in the "successful" states did no better than keep up with the level of inflation (19 percent) during this period. In ten of the eleven "successful" states, wage levels actually fell below the national average (and, compared with the "unsuccessful" states, were one-seventh lower for overall wages and one-sixth lower for manufacturing wages). In only one state (California) did wage level increases surpass the annual national average. There they did so by a little less than 0.5 percent. On the other hand, seventeen of the thirty-seven states in the "unsuccessful" category experienced wage increases above the national average, although they lacked economic development programs that effectively accelerated the rate of growth of new jobs. On the whole, the efforts of states to create economic development programs and to generate large numbers of new jobs have failed to bring about higher real wages.

Like the states, some cities have been more fortunate than others in discovering and implementing economic development strategies. Yet even these have had little more success in alleviating the problems of the working poor. This conclusion is underlined by the experiences of a number of cities to which my community looked when we developed our economic strategy. We focused on the strategies of four cities around the nation—Charlotte, North Carolina; Columbus, Ohio; Fort Worth, Texas; and Portland, Oregon—all of which were similar in size to our city and considered highly effective in business and economic development.[13] At the end of the recession, in 1983, to 1990, each of these cities

Table 17

STATES WITH ECONOMIC DEVELOPMENT PROGRAMS, JOB INCREASES ABOVE THE NATIONAL AVERAGE IN MANUFACTURING JOBS OR OVERALL JOBS, AND WAGE INCREASES, 1984–1989 (IN PERCENTAGES)

State	Increase in Overall Jobs	Increase in Manufacturing Jobs	Annual Increase in Wages above or below National Average
Nevada	36.9 (23.9)*	20.5	−0.32
Arizona	24.7 (11.7)	8.5	−0.72
California	19.4 (6.4)	4.7	0.44
Michigan	17.7 (4.7)	1.9	−0.86
Indiana	17.3 (4.3)	4.2	−1.18
Utah	15.7 (2.7)	9.7	−2.04
Minnesota	14.3 (1.3)	7.0	−0.02
Wisconsin	14.3 (1.3)	7.7	−0.78
Ohio	13.9 (0.9)	−0.5	−1.14
Iowa	11.0 (−2.0)	10.0	−1.06
North Dakota	3.1 (−9.9)	6.3	−2.40

* The figures in parentheses represent the gain or loss in employment compared with the national average. Similar figures are not given for manufacturing employment, since nationally there was no net change in manufacturing jobs.

Source: U.S. Department of Labor, Bureau of Labor Statistics, *Employment and Earnings: Annual Averages,* vol. 32–37 (1985–90).

equaled or surpassed the national average in the generation of new jobs. Three of the four significantly reduced their rate of unemployment, and the fourth did as well toward the end of the period. Nevertheless, the data available for these cities on per capita income and wages show at best a mixed picture. The growth in per capita income in two of these cities failed to match the growth in the nation as a whole. The third city, Columbus, managed only to keep even with national growth in income, despite a 44 percent increase in the number of new jobs between 1983 and 1988. Only Charlotte surpassed the national rate of income growth (by about 1.7 percent a year during the period). Looking at increases in manufacturing wages—purported to be the highest—we find that in Fort Worth, the city with the greatest growth in new jobs, the real average hourly wage rate

Table 18
UNEMPLOYMENT RATES (IN PERCENTAGES)

	1983	1984	1985	1986	1987	1988	1989	1990
Charlotte	8.1	5.2	4.4	5.1	3.9	3.1	3.0	3.0
Fort Worth	5.8	3.9	4.7	5.9	6.3	7.0	5.2	4.5
Columbus	9.5	8.1	7.1	5.8	5.8	6.1	4.7	4.7
Portland	11.5	9.0	8.6	7.9	5.6	5.3	4.4	4.1
National Average	10.1	7.7	7.2	7.2	6.6	5.6	5.0	5.2

Source: U.S. Department of Labor, Bureau of Labor Statistics, *Employment and Earnings* 31–38, no. 5 (May 1983–91): table D-1.

Table 19
PERCENTAGE GROWTH IN
PERSONAL INCOME, PER CAPITA,
1983–1988

Columbus	37.7
Charlotte	45.2
Fort Worth	26.9
Portland	32.0
National Average	36.5

Source: U.S. Department of Commerce, Bureau of Economic Analysis, *Local Area Personal Income* 1 (1990): 84–170.

Table 20
AVERAGE HOURLY EARNINGS IN MANUFACTURING (IN DOLLARS)

	1985	1986	1987	1988	1989	1990	Percentage Change 1985–1990
Fort Worth	9.30	9.47	9.94	10.48	10.88	11.18	20.2
Columbus	10.88	11.13	11.46	11.75	11.84	12.39	13.9
Portland	10.37	10.74	10.86	10.96	10.89	11.22	8.2
Charlotte	7.30	7.61	7.98	8.29	8.78	9.21	26.1
National Consumer Price Index							19.6

Source: U.S. Department of Labor, Bureau of Labor Statistics, *Employment and Earnings* 32–38, no. 5 (May 1984–91): Tables C-8.

only kept pace with the consumer price index. Despite substantial new-job creation in two of the cities, Columbus and Portland, real wage rates actually fell when compared with increases in the consumer price index. Only in Charlotte did hourly wages better the price index, by 1.5 percent per year.[14]

In my discussions with colleagues around the nation, I learned that few, if any, tools available at the local level actually raise wages. Most cities complement their economic development programs with two other strategies that attempt directly to improve the quality of the wages accessible to their citizens. One strategy attempted in numerous communities involves the competition for quality employees that exists between the public and the private sectors. Using this strategy, the local government acts as the wage leader by setting the standard for better wages through its own employment practices. The assumption guiding this strategy is that the private sector will eventually follow suit as the best in the employee pool gravitate toward government. Virtually all fellow mayors whom I surveyed agreed that the government's setting community standards for wages through its own work force was important for their communities, although not one mayor was able to document the actual impact this "leadership" strategy had on private-sector wages.

The national movement for privatization of numerous functions typically performed by public-sector employees threatens further to reduce the real wages of at least those employees and to swell the ranks of the working poor. For example, if a city ceases garbage collection and allows private-sector firms to take over this activity, the employees who will leave the city payroll may be fortunate to find the same jobs in the private sector. Yet if they do, they will be working for wages up to 50 percent less than those in the public sector. Nor will they receive the type of health benefits provided by the municipal government. For them and their families, life will grow harsher. To my knowledge, there is not a single case nationwide where "privatization" of municipal services has not led to a reduction in wages and benefits in the community.[15]

Job training is a second strategy that municipal governments use to address the problem of low wages. Many of the men and women in the cities of our nation who toil for very low wages have good skills and histories of better-paying jobs. A skilled copper miner cannot easily transfer his skills to become a computer programmer. Without training, the only option is usually unskilled service jobs. Job-training programs are often seen as critically important to municipalities that are interested in providing their citizens a better opportunity for decent-paying jobs. In fact, all but four of the fifty states have aggressively pursued state-funded, customized training programs for their citizens,[16] in addition to the job-training resources made available by municipalities.

Unfortunately, although job-training programs are vital for economic development, they are no panacea. Part of the problem is the scarcity of local resources for the effort. Most cities are reeling from major reductions in federal funding for job training. My city is typical. Fifteen years ago, we received $15 million in federal job-training assistance. Today, federal assistance totals just $5 million. No new employer that we have attracted in three years came with its own full complement of job-training capabilities. In virtually every case, job training was part of the package of incentives we provided to prospective employers. In the vast majority of cases, precious job-training resources led to job opportunities for our citizens both in manufacturing and in service positions with "competitive" wage rates often no higher than $5.50 to $6.50 an hour. While we found some resources to give our citizens a chance to train themselves for new jobs, we were nevertheless unable to have much impact on the quality of wages in the community with this strategy. Cities throughout the nation have had the same experience. Job training, in and of itself, cannot significantly alleviate the wage problem in the community unless high-wage jobs are available to workers.

THE CONSEQUENCES OF LOW WAGES

The immediate consequences of low wages are felt throughout the community. When families struggle on the margins of the economy and have virtually no latitude in their budgets, even minor new financial burdens can upset the precarious balance. For example, events in the Persian Gulf increased gasoline prices in our city by twenty cents a gallon for a few months. The burden of this increase for those living below self-sufficiency quickly became manifest. The rise in fuel costs meant an added expenditure of only about four dollars a week to the average family. Yet, within a month, gasoline sales fell and ridership on our public transportation system increased by 15 percent. A twenty-cent rise in the price at the gas pump helped us meet a goal for the usage of mass transit that we had reached only once before, and then only after twelve months of intensive advertising. Similar results were reported in most cities with active transportation systems.

The effects of low-wage employment are most striking when one examines the quality of housing. In our city, with unemployment significantly below the national and state average, large numbers of families nevertheless live on the margins of affordable housing. In a metropolitan area of about 250,000 families, 25,000 families are estimated to have substandard housing. Two thousand families are on the waiting list for public housing, but the list is deceptive: we cap the list at 2,000 so that we will not create false expectations for those additional families in need who also seek to get on the list. The alternative to public housing assistance is to stay with friends or family in overcrowded living conditions. Fred, who is thirty-two and has a wife and two children, called me three times in one week. He was looking for public housing. The last time he called, he blurted out, "I never dreamed that I would have a full-time job and be forced to have my family live with my parents in a two-bedroom apartment. What a cruel joke this is!"

Homeless families, who face a dramatically more difficult situation, are likely to have to remain on the streets even when low-paying jobs are available. To move into an apartment, most families will need around $1,000 for the first month's rent, the last month's rent, and the security deposit, not including the deposits for utilities. For most, who have no savings, $1,000 is a princely sum that wages of $5, $6, or $7 an hour do not enable them to raise. In many instances, families cannot afford the actual rents on these wages.

The absence of economic self-sufficiency has its most vicious effects within the family. The frustrations of working to make ends meet and never quite being able to do so often leads to domestic conflict and violence. Every three months, I would go out with police officers on their regular beat. At least once a night, we encountered a case of domestic violence, with spouse attacking spouse, or adult attacking child. In many, though not all, of these cases, the arguments stem from lack of money for clothes or entertainment and often result in violence. Our shelters for battered women and children are overfilled with people not just from the poorest of our citizens but, just as likely, from those living at or near the margins of our economy.

The darker side of life in the world of underpaid workers often is seen as well in inadequate child care and the frustrations that it can cause. When both mother and father work and manage to scrape together enough only for survival, another cruel irony awaits: neither can afford to stay at home, neither can raise the children, and even with both parents working, they cannot afford child care. A fortunate few have other family members willing to lend a hand. Yet even here the misery and frustration is spread to parents, who may no longer be able to help. Take the case of Ellen, who was distressed enough to call my office. She is fifty-seven and crippled by arthritis. She wanted me to help her find child care for her two granddaughters, whose parents both work. "They can't afford to take them anywhere but to me," she said. "And I can't handle it any more. Isn't it enough that I raised two kids myself?" And then she asked, "Am I a bad person for feeling like this?"

Ellen's grandchildren are lucky. A number of their counterparts are every day left at home alone, or worse. A recent newspaper article reported the trial and conviction of one woman who, while working at a second job on Saturdays, dressed her daughter in pajamas and locked her in the trunk of her car in a shopping mall parking lot. At the hearing to determine her fitness as a parent, she testified before the judge that she couldn't afford day care and that both she and her daughter would starve without the second job.

The lack of economic opportunity affects every part of society. Schoolteachers in our public schools complain of the lack of parents' interest in their children's education. "My kids lack the motivation to learn," said one teacher at a school in a low-income neighborhood, "and I can motivate them somewhat, but they receive none of the motivation at home. But it's even worse than that, because once I meet the parents, I can't even blame them for it. Most of the parents I meet, they are so caught up in their own daily survival, they are too exhausted, and they are too bitter about life to motivate their kids as well. I can't blame them for their apathy."

Yet, clearly, she cannot motivate her students by herself. And the results are obvious. The dropout rate in the high schools from our lower-income families is reaching epidemic proportions. Inside the classroom, one can feel the bitterness, hostility, and alienation of sixteen-year-olds who live in futureless families. "Get a high school degree?" one said to me, smiling a bittersweet smile. "And then what? My parents *are* high school graduates!"

When wages are low and families are struggling, there can be little expectation that citizens will invest in upgrading their community. Bond proposals designed to create better conditions for learning in our schools have failed three consecutive times. Despite the widespread recognition that our schools need more resources to educate our children well, many of our citizens feel that they cannot bear the added burden.

Cities and states throughout the nation are struggling to improve the economic conditions for all citizens, including the working poor. None has effectively solved the problem yet. Meanwhile, the suffering and despair continue. It is clearly not a lack of caring that is responsible. Every conceivable economic strategy has been tried. Although some advances have occurred, in and of themselves local jurisdictions simply have not been able to find the tools that can succeed in providing most of the working poor with better job opportunities and a decent standard of living. It is necessary to recognize that effective solutions to working poverty will not and cannot come from the state and local levels alone. They must be found elsewhere.

THE PATH OF ACTION

Although the Americans who have been the focus of this book come from nearly every kind of socioeconomic and educational background, they have one thing in common. They are unable to provide adequately for their families by practicing the work ethic. They either work full-time the entire year and remain poor or work at lesser levels, unable to find full-time employment that is sufficiently steady and well-paying to lift them out of poverty. We frequently hear that the number of Americans receiving welfare is large. Even during years of sustained economic growth, as in 1989, working poverty strikes the lives of nearly twelve million workers, and almost thirty million persons if their families are included, affecting nearly three times as many Americans as are on welfare at any one time.[1] Over the past half century the nation has struggled to find solutions, at the federal as well as at the state and local levels. Nevertheless, the problem of working poverty persists.

Indeed, our present policies to assist the poor create another grave injustice that ought not be ignored—namely, that Americans who work full-time the whole year frequently end up with incomes at or beneath the level that public assistance grants to many welfare recipients who are employed intermittently or not at all. In 1989, the median assistance that a recipient could receive from welfare was itself on the frugal side; the value of the entire package of welfare benefits, received by approximately one-third of all welfare recipients, was about 20 percent beneath the threshold of self-sufficiency.[2] For a family of three, this amount would require a fully employed person who received no governmental assistance to work at $6.50 an hour in order to obtain the same after-tax income. About 18 percent of the jobs held by fully employed Americans in 1989 paid less than this. Nearly three and a half million workers fully employed throughout 1989 did in fact reside in households with incomes that were lower than the median value of the package available from welfare for a family of their size. So did another two million workers who were usually employed full-time. About two million more lived on incomes that surpassed these benefits by no more than 15 percent.

All these workers (and other persons who decided not to work) found themselves in what is often called the poverty trap. This trap refers to the circumstance in which public assistance grants welfare recipients nearly as much income as, or possibly even more than, they would earn by working. Sandra Bolton's bitter inner conflict over whether she should quit work and take welfare or sell drugs—a conflict the mere mention of which left her in tears—attests to its insidious influence. That she and many other workers decide to become and remain employed even though continuing to be poor testifies to their commitment to the work ethic.

Though unintended, the effect of the nation's present policy is to say that the work of these people has no meaning that translates into any discernible economic reward beyond what is available from welfare. The fully employed in 1989 who earned incomes roughly equal to the median assistance from welfare made our clothes and the flag we honor. They built furniture for our homes and helped construct those homes. They turned out precision products that we use in our offices. They worked in our hospitals and cared for our children. They managed sections and departments in our stores. They took care of the elderly in nursing homes. They planted and harvested our food. They cleaned our places of work and our schools.

That public assistance frequently pays as much as full-time employment has been pointed out by many critics of welfare. They believe that welfare benefits should be reduced, in fairness to those who work and to give incentives to those who do not. However, this provides no solution. The real problem is not high welfare benefits but low wages. Reducing welfare benefits would still leave fully employed workers who are poor with their present inadequate earnings, all of them beneath economic self-sufficiency.

In addition, most families on public assistance, like those of the fully employed, contain children. A main objective of public assistance is to make sure that children have a roof over their heads, heat in their homes, a minimally nutritious diet, and health care. The median welfare standard in the nation for those who receive the entire package of welfare programs is now about 80 percent of the threshold of self-sufficiency.[3] It falls to beneath 60 percent of self-sufficiency for the nearly two-thirds of welfare recipients who get no housing assistance. Compared with the realistic cost of purchasing the basic necessities, the median welfare assistance is not excessive.[4] It could certainly not be lowered significantly and still provide adequate protection. The poverty trap, then, does not exist primarily because welfare benefits are too high. The predicament is instead one more symptom of the deeper problem, the scarcity of decent-paying jobs. Relative to the cost of meeting necessities, too many of the jobs for fully employed workers pay too little.

It compounds this problem that the present welfare system does not actually focus on rewarding the work ethic of the low-income population. Welfare instead concentrates its efforts on assisting those among the poor who do not work or who work intermittently. The nation's social policies concentrate on low-income people who are not fully employed. They offer less attention and comparatively meager benefits to Americans who *do* work, but for low wages. They tend to assume that people who are fully employed are in an economic position to take care of themselves, and to forget how badly off many of these workers are. The unhappy result of these policies is to leave many low-income Americans who work full-time the entire year no better, or even worse, off economically than recipients of welfare. This needs to end.

Ronald Reagan saw the problem: "It is time to reform this outdated social dinosaur and finally break the poverty trap," he said, in regard to the welfare system.[5] Yet we can do so only by traveling down the opposite path from the one that the former president would have the nation take. The only effective path is to make certain that long, hard work yields a meaningful return. A key flaw in the present system is that public assistance is ultimately judged by whether it gets people to seek, find, and take employment and not by whether it assures workers who are fully employed that their basic needs will be met. For public assistance to succeed, it must pay the same attention to the rewards of employment as to employment itself. The way out is for the nation to act consistently with the precepts of the American ethos and commit itself to the policy that every person who is fully employed[6] will have the means to afford the basic necessities at a minimally decent level. This is the goal of the program we will propose. It should, at a minimum, be the goal of the nation.[7] Given the American faith that work will be rewarded, fully employed workers deserve no less.

Although the government has tended to concentrate upon

the poor who are not fully employed, it has not entirely ignored the needs of the working poor and their rewards from work. Ever since the New Deal, the government has recognized that low pay is a problem. Though it has vastly understated the scale and generally misdiagnosed the nature of the problem, it has implemented some policies to help low-wage workers that can be adapted to the goal of attaining minimally adequate incomes for all fully employed workers. It is best to work with existing policies, for it is a political fact of life that Congress is more apt to alter present policies than to approve completely new policy approaches.

The policies most relevant to reform are the minimum wage and the special tax credits for low-wage workers now in our tax system, called the Earned Income Tax Credit. The goal that all fully employed workers in America be enabled to afford basic necessities can be achieved by interconnecting, coordinating, and strengthening these policies. It requires, first, a moderate increase in the minimum wage and, second, an expansion of the special tax credits for fully employed workers in a manner tied directly to the threshold of self-sufficiency. These actions will be effective for all fully employed workers who are at present covered by health insurance through their place of employment. A series of other proposals is now before Congress to assure affordable health insurance for workers who currently have none. Enactment of our proposal together with insurance reform will enable all fully employed workers to have incomes allowing them to reach a minimally decent standard of living.

The economy budget described in chapter 3 sets forth the income, relative to the official poverty line, that workers realistically need in order to be able to afford basic necessities. Approximating this income for 1991, we find that a household of one would need $10,900; a household of two,

$13,600; a household of three, $16,600; and a household of four, $21,300.[8]

A new minimum wage, by itself, can give fully employed workers without children the income they need. The minimum wage cannot mean anything less than a wage enabling a single person without children, working moderately longer than the standard workweek (say, forty-five hours a week), to attain self-sufficiency.[9] The minimum wage should not be lower than this. A new minimum wage of $4.85 an hour would enable a worker employed for these hours to earn $10,900 over a year, or self-sufficiency for a single person (the present minimum wage is $4.25 an hour). If working a standard forty-hour workweek, a person would need a wage of about $5.50 an hour (about 15 percent above the new minimum wage) to attain the $10,900 self-sufficiency income.

The minimum wage can thus provide the income needed for self-sufficiency for all fully employed households without children. It must be coupled, however, with some type of income supplement if fully employed families with children—families like the Lamberts, the Bartelles, and the Boltons—are to have a similar prospect.[10]

America has already taken steps to offer earnings supplements to working households with children. Congress first enacted what is called the Earned Income Tax Credit (EITC) in 1975 and has enlarged it several times since. Through the EITC, the government gives payments to workers with incomes beneath a certain specified amount. The program operates through the normal tax system and thus requires little new bureaucracy. Equally important, it respects the privacy of the individual, unlike many welfare programs that often publicly stigmatize recipients. Americans who receive earnings supplements through tax credits fill out tax returns and enjoy the same privacy of these tax returns as do all other taxpayers.

In 1990, the EITC granted a 14 percent credit to workers

for each dollar of earnings, up to annual earnings of $6,810 for a family, thereby providing a maximum additional supplement of $953 to the family. The credit remained at $953 until the family's annual earnings reached $10,730, after which it declined at a rate of 10 percent for each additional dollar earned. So, if a family earned $15,730, its credit was $453, raising its income to $16,183. The credit returned to zero when family earnings reached $20,264.

Current law also provides for an expansion of the EITC each year until 1994. Projections for the 1992 tax year are that the minimum credit for a family with two or more children be $1,332 for incomes at $10,000 and about $320 for incomes at $20,000.[11] Even with this assistance, however, families of two adults and two children would still remain beneath self-sufficiency (an income of about $22,000 in 1992) unless and until they attained about $21,850 in earnings.

A rather similar program of sliding tax credits would provide the possibility for self-sufficiency to all fully employed families with children. Let us start, once again, with people who are employed at the minimum wage and consider the case of a family with two adults and two children. Suppose that the family has one worker at the new minimum wage ($4.85 an hour) and one half-time worker earning the same wage. The chief wage earner is employed for forty hours a week throughout the year on one or a combination of jobs and the second earner for half that much. This is the maximum the proposal expects parents with children to work.[12] Working at the minimum wage for the whole year, the parents together earn about $15,100 before taxes, or about $13,700 after taxes.[13] In 1991, however, the income a family of four realistically needed for basic necessities came to approximately $21,300 before taxes, or about $18,200 after taxes. This $18,200 threshold of self-sufficiency, after taxes, stands $4,500 higher than the family's actual after-tax income of $13,700. There is thus a deficiency of $4,500 between

Table 21

EARNINGS SUPPLEMENTS AND TAXES FOR FULLY EMPLOYED FAMILIES OF FOUR AT DIFFERENT
INCOME LEVELS (IN DOLLARS)

Family Income	Supplement	Total Income before Tax	Tax[a]	Net Tax Payment[b]	Total Income after Tax
15,100	4,500	19,600	1,410	− 3,090	18,190
17,100	4,000	21,100	1,860	− 2,140	19,240
21,700	2,850	24,550	2,890	+ 40	21,660
27,000	1,525	28,525	4,070	+ 2,545	24,455

[a] Based on federal income and Social Security taxes as of the 1990 tax year.
[b] The net tax payment is the difference between the tax and the supplement.

the family's income and the income required for self-sufficiency.

The program would grant a tax credit equal to this deficiency. That is, the credit would bridge the gap between a fully employed family's income, working at the minimum wage, and a self-sufficiency income. For fully employed families of four with two adults and two children, the credit would achieve this result for all who reached the basic $15,100 income level.[14]

As family income rose beyond $15,100, the credit would decline by 25 percent for each additional dollar of income, until the credit was phased out. For example, a family with a gross income that was $2,000 higher (that is, $17,100) would lose $500 of the credit, leaving a credit of $4,000 (see table 21). This would produce a total income of $21,100. After taxes were paid on the original gross income, the family's after-tax income would be about $19,240.

The tax credit, then, would enable all fully employed families to attain self-sufficiency.[15] At a gross income slightly above self-sufficiency—$21,700, for a family of four—the credit would turn into a reduction in the taxes the family owes. For a family with this $21,700 income, the federal taxes the family owed ($2,890) would surpass the credit

($2,850), leaving a small tax payment, as table 21 shows. At a gross income one-quarter higher, $27,000, the credit would have declined to $1,525. In this case, the family would end up paying taxes of $2,545, instead of the $4,070 in taxes it would otherwise owe, resulting in a tax reduction of $1,525.

To do otherwise—that is, to set the credits so that when they are coupled with earnings no family could receive any more than a self-sufficiency income after taxes—would have the effect of placing many fully employed families in a 100 percent tax bracket. All of these families would receive the same self-sufficiency income after taxes—$18,200—no matter how much they had earned. If we took this path, with our first two examples, the family earning $17,100 would end up receiving the same after-tax income of $18,200 as the family earning $15,100. Indeed, anyone earning up to $21,300 would receive $18,200 after taxes. This, obviously, cannot be the appropriate policy. However, no other alternative exists if we decide that tax reductions cannot go to families who are above self-sufficiency. It is either that or doing nothing at all and leaving the working poor in their present grim circumstances, with the many grave injustices and disincentives to work that this entails.

Some Americans find little problem with the idea of helping poor families if it means extending tax relief to families above self-sufficiency as well. These are all hardworking families, and the self-sufficiency budget is so frugal that even families living modestly above it often have to struggle to make ends meet. Evidence suggests that as many as one-third of the families with incomes of up to 200 percent of the official poverty line (equal to nearly $28,000 for a family of four in 1991) are unable to afford food, clothing, or medical care at some time during the year.[16] It appears that some 40 percent of the families at this same income level and somewhat beyond, to about $34,000 in 1991 dollars, may have too little income to pay for their shelter, coupled with all the other expenses of households with children.[17]

The costs of raising children are so burdensome that dozens of bills now lie before Congress to give families with children help by raising the tax deduction for children or by providing substantial tax credits for children. Democrats and Republicans alike have introduced these proposals. We will discuss the relative merits of these proposals and ours below.[18] What is relevant here is that not one of the bills confines its benefits to poor families. Every proposal would make the larger deductions and credits available to middle- and even upper-income families as well. In this regard, the program we have proposed is much more focused. The top eligible gross income that a family of four could have and still receive any tax relief on the sliding scale our proposal contains is about $33,000—well below the nation's median income for these families. Indeed, if it were concluded that a broader range of families ought to have greater tax relief, our proposal could serve as a suitable vehicle by simply extending its tax reductions at some specified level to families beyond the income ceiling that it now sets.[19]

Through our program, a family like the Bartelles would receive tax credits totaling about $2,800, help they desperately need. With this added income, they would no longer have to eat potatoes or potatoes and eggs for several days running in order to pay late shelter and utility bills; they could purchase clothes for themselves and their children; they could keep their car in decent repair; they could buy furniture for their living room to replace worn couches that now leave them feeling ashamed; and they could begin to put away money for the time, soon approaching, when they will need to replace their roofing. Or consider the Boltons. Sandra and her family would receive about $2,600 in tax credits. She would then have enough money for food without having to sell her blood or having to work fifty or fifty-five hours a week while trying to raise two children; she could afford shoes for her children; she could buy a bed for herself, rather than having to sleep on the floor, and get furniture for her living room; she could afford to get dental care and braces and a retainer for her youngest son, Matt, without relying on gifts from others; and she might, after all these years, qualify for a home loan.

This policy commitment would not merely improve the lives of the fully employed poor. It would also change the conditions that face workers like Ray Clark who are now employed part-time or less because they cannot find full-time jobs with adequate wages. With the enactment of a policy that effectively supplements the low earnings of fully employed workers, full-time jobs that were previously refused because their meager wages would leave families still in dire need, and less well off than would welfare or crime,[20] would now generate significantly higher earnings. The jobs would thus become more realistic alternatives to welfare or crime. This policy would have made a decisive difference in the life of Ray Clark and his family.

Moreover, many other low-wage families, even those containing infants or very small children, escaped poverty only because both parents were gainfully employed. In 1990, the median hourly wage for all production and nonsupervisory workers (composing about four-fifths of all private-sector workers in America) was $10.02. Employed at this wage, a year-round full-time worker earned barely enough to reach the threshold of self-sufficiency ($20,658) for a family of four during that year. Almost 25 percent of all year-round full-time workers were unable to earn even three-quarters of this amount. This is to say that having a family of two parents and two children with one parent gainfully employed and one at home was not an option available to a large segment of the work force in the United States if they wanted to escape poverty, not even if there were preschool children in their family. By making special provision for households with small children, our proposal would enable families earning these wages to attain self-sufficiency with one fully employed worker, thus offering the parents a choice they do not now have.

Apart from that of making ends meet, another serious problem confronts families with fully employed parents. Low-wage workers who are fully employed and want to improve their education frequently feel unable to do so. Some are unable because they think they cannot afford to cut back on work and lose income. They may also feel that when their jobs are coupled with their roles as parent and spouse, they have neither enough time nor enough energy left to pursue further education on a sustained basis. The proposed program could help low-wage earners with children gain access to educational opportunities and improve their skills by offering them an option. Fully employed workers who cut back their hours of employment up to a certain maximum (say, 25 percent) in order to earn educational credits representing one-quarter time or more in an accredited program could be permitted to continue receiving the tax credits, and thus be treated just as if they were still fully employed.

Consider the head of a family of four who returned to school part-time and whose employer arranged for him to drop down to three-quarters time on the job. Suppose, too, that the earnings of the head were $12,000 and those of the second earner $6,000, resulting in a gross income of $18,000. By working three-quarters time, the head of the family would lower his earnings to $9,000. This would reduce the family's gross income to $15,000. However, as table 22 shows, the various supplements on an income of $15,000 for a family of four would add $4,525 to the income, which would leave an after-tax income of just over $18,100. This is more than $2,000 higher than the after-tax income the family now has on earnings of $18,000 without the supplement program, as table 22 indicates. In addition, the after-tax income of $18,100 would enable the family to stay near the threshold of self-sufficiency.

Table 22

THE EFFECT OF THE ABSENCE OF A SUPPLEMENT PROGRAM AND CONTINUATION OF THE SUPPLEMENT PROGRAM ON FAMILIES IN WHICH A FULLY EMPLOYED WORKER REDUCES WORK HOURS BY ONE-QUARTER FOR EDUCATIONAL PURPOSES (IN DOLLARS) [a]

No Supplement Program			Continuation of the Supplement Program			
Family Income	Tax[b]	Total Income after Tax	Family Income	Supplement	Tax[b]	Total Income after Tax
18,000	2,060	15,940	18,000	3,775	2,060	19,715
15,000	1,390	13,610	15,000	4,525	1,390	18,135

[a] Calculations are based on a family of four.
[b] Based on federal income and Social Security taxes as of the 1990 tax year.

The supplements proposed here for fully employed workers and their families would replace all programs currently available to full-time working persons save for those relating to health benefits and child care. Fully employed persons who took the supplements would become ineligible for food stamps, school lunch, housing assistance, energy assistance, and other such programs. If the proposed program did indeed provide households with a reasonable prospect of obtaining incomes sufficient to meet necessities, the other programs would become redundant. Moreover, many of the present programs, whether that is their intention or not, publicly stigmatize recipients, an unconscionable thing to do to fully employed people. The new program, implemented through the privacy of the normal tax system, would remove this stigma.

The benefits of this program to fully employed families would be numerous. Improvements in their condition, in turn, will promote the resolution of other issues facing the nation. For example, it is hard to imagine that any policy to reduce welfare dependency or crime can make much headway as long as employment does not offer a path enabling people to afford the basic necessities. Working poverty also compounds the problem of raising educational standards. The children from these families often go to school suffering from hunger or illness, which lessens their ability to concentrate. Their lack of access to educational tools that are available to children in the homes of families with more income to spare further erodes their educational advancement, as does the underfunding of many of their schools. Not even the nation's economic performance is surely immune from the effects of the prevalence of low wages and the scant purchasing power of millions of working people, for these have possibly acted as a brake on the vitality and overall growth of the economy.

At the same time, there may be reservations about the size and scale of the program we are proposing. In the remainder of this chapter, we will explore questions related to the cost and affordability of the program. Appendix A at the end of the book examines a series of other possible economic objections.

It should be noted that the direct costs would go beyond the cost of the benefits themselves. There would be administrative costs, too, both to private businesses and to the government. Employers would need to provide the government with yearly figures regarding the hours their employees worked (as they now provide yearly figures on earnings, health insurance benefits, and payroll tax deductions). For its part, the Internal Revenue Service would need to store the new information and apply it to individual tax returns.

A substantially larger cost, however, involves the benefits. Raising the minimum wage, as we propose, would affect the labor costs of employers and lead, some would argue, to a reduction of jobs. We believe that this effect would be small. The proposal contains a modest increase in the minimum wage of 14 percent and thereby returns the minimum wage to its historical level relative to the average hourly wage that it held in the 1950s, 1960s, and 1970s.[21] That is, the minimum-wage level the proposal contains existed during a time that all agree was one of strong economic growth—the 1950s and 1960s. Moreover, even the so-called weak economy of the 1970s generated 20.6 million new jobs. During the 1980s, when there was hardly any increase in the minimum wage, the economy created 18.3 million new jobs, 2 million fewer than in the 1970s.

The tax credits are another matter, however. Their cost, though hard to predict precisely, would be large. Predictions are hazardous partly because it is impossible to know how many eligible people would take advantage of the program. This so-called take-up rate varies greatly among different programs and sometimes even for the same program in different years.[22] We cannot know, either, how many families currently headed by unemployed or partly employed workers would become eligible because they decided to accept year-round full-time work, which the program would give people every incentive to do. The program would enable people to earn discernibly more through full-time work than they can currently receive from welfare.

Presume, as an extreme, that after the program's enactment nearly all the twelve million workers who are potentially eligible do become eligible and in fact apply. This would amount to about nine million households.[23] Assume, too, that the average tax supplement package for these nine million households is $3,000 (the largest possible supplement for an eligible family of four in which both adults were working[24] at the new minimum wage would be $4,500).[25] The cost in tax credits, then, would amount to about $27 billion a year. In addition, households with incomes above self-sufficiency would receive tax reductions of about $6 billion,[26] resulting in an overall cost of $33 billion.

For those taking the supplements, the proposed program would replace all existing programs (except child care and health care assistance) for which these families would otherwise be eligible, including the present Earned Income Tax Credit. For these fully employed families, the EITC alone would total around $3 billion today and $5 billion by 1994. Moreover, some of the families that are now unemployed or partly unemployed but that would become fully employed because of the new program may at present be on AFDC or unemployment. Many may also be getting assistance from food stamps, housing programs, and other income or in-kind subsidies. Since we do not know exactly who or even how many these families would be, no firm estimate is possible. A conservative estimate is that, if they totaled four million, the households would be receiving about $8 billion at present (an average of $2,000 for each household)—which, added to the aforementioned $5 billion, would come to $13 billion. Since the proposed program would expend a projected $33 billion a year on these households, the difference between present policies and the new program would amount to an estimated $20 billion a year. This is the cost to purchase for Americans the assurance that with hard work and perseverance they can all afford the basic necessities.

Is this cost—$20 billion—beyond the nation's means? The government currently plans to reduce military spending by one-quarter, or $75 billion a year, by the end of the century. Were it to do so by only half this sum ($38 billion), the proposed program would cost about half of the savings from the cut in defense expenditures.

It is well to remember, too, that the federal budget is not stationary even when there is no tax hike. New revenue flows to the budget as the economy grows in real terms. From 1980 to 1990, the nation experienced a 31 percent rate of real economic growth, not an unusual performance. The economy averaged about this same rate of real growth even in the 1970s, supposedly a decade with a sluggish economy, and also in the last half of the 1960s. Thanks mostly to the economic growth, the federal government's general revenue (minus Social Security taxes) grew by a real 15 percent from 1980 to 1990. By 1990, the annual revenues of the federal government, excluding Social Security, were $94 billion higher in 1990 dollars than they had been in 1980. Suppose that annual federal revenues grow by only three-quarters of this amount during the 1990s, or $70 billion. In this case, the nation could fund the estimated $20 billion cost of the proposed program by use of one-third of the growth in governmental revenues, and it could do so with no increase in taxes. Indeed, if we add the defense reduction of $38 billion to the rise in federal revenues of $70 billion, the government would then have $108 billion in available revenues, or greater than five times the estimated cost of the proposed program. The basic belief that hard work should gain every person a place at the table in America will be an ideal of little real value to the nation if we are unwilling to fulfill its promise to fully employed American workers by paying even this small price.

The program we have proposed, in fact, provides a way to attack working poverty that would be substantially less expensive than proposals at present before Congress. The most common of these other proposals, seemingly similar to ours, would grant increased tax deductions, or establish new tax credits, for families with children. This tax assistance would apply to all households with children. Consider a proposal that would grant a $1,000 tax credit for every child in the household under the age of eighteen, to replace the far smaller deductions for children that the tax system now allows. Because the proposal would apply equally to all households at all income levels, the net cost to the Treasury would amount to about $40 billion a year, twice the cost of our proposal. Moreover, this additional $40 billion in tax assistance would still leave many families beneath self-sufficiency. For example, if $2,000 in tax credits were given to a family with two children, a family of four with an income as high as even $18,500 would have an after-tax income of about $17,700, still about $500 beneath the needed $18,200 self-sufficiency income after taxes. Families earning $15,000 a year would be left nearly $3,000 beneath the needed after-tax income.

An additional problem with these proposals before Congress is that they do not differentiate between working and nonworking families. All households with children would receive the credit, whether the adults were working or not. Workers' income relative to nonworkers' would thus continue to be the same under these proposals as it is now. That means the proposals fail to attack one of the most pernicious social problems the nation faces: the poverty trap. Unlike these proposals, ours would not only lift all fully employed families to self-sufficiency, and accomplish this goal with far less expense, but also dismantle the poverty trap.

The goal of enabling all fully employed households in America to achieve incomes meeting the threshold of self-sufficiency or beyond reaches to the deepest roots of American thinking—to our belief in reciprocity, to our respect for the values of hard work, perseverance, and responsibility, and to our ethos that all who practice these values, no matter what their background or station, will gain a decent livelihood. These are ideas that all Americans embrace.

For about twenty years now, the span of an entire generation, the nation's story has been one of success on the international rather than on the domestic front. The successful completion of the Cold War has been a highly significant achievement. On the other hand, there has been little progress at home to give Americans a feeling of pride as a nation for all these years. Nor has there been much consensus among us upon which to build. Assuring that all fully employed Americans have minimally adequate incomes or better can help bring to the nation a renewed sense of common purpose. The achievement of this goal will place the nation once more on the sound footing of the American ethos. It will simultaneously help it move more effectively toward other goals. By taking up and meeting this challenge, the nation will light a beacon of hope that historically has been part of the very idea and meaning of this land—not simply to our own people but to people at the farthest reaches of the globe.

EPILOGUE
A Call for Action

We have seen that the idea that work enables people to become self-sufficient is a myth, even during favorable economic times, for thirty million Americans. Their suffering results from a scarcity of decent-paying jobs. Compelling justifications to provide a remedy derive not only from the premise of the American ethos but also from the social contract idea upon which our nation is based. We have proposed a remedy that is workable. Yet workable remedies and sound moral justifications, even when rooted in the nation's most deeply cherished values, are not always sufficient to bring about action. Action ultimately depends upon the political system, and the political system depends upon elected officials. Elected officials, no matter how noble, are not likely to take action if doing so, in their view, might cause them serious political harm. In this day and age, when American voters are widely thought to be profoundly skeptical of governmental activism, will a program be politically feasible if it calls for a more activist federal stance in the area of social policy? Will advocacy of such a program not prove to be an electoral liability?

In this epilogue, we examine the most important political objections to a comprehensive program to assist low-income working Americans. We show that, far from being a liability, a sound program to assist the working poor has the potential to be an important electoral asset.

Imagine that you are sitting in your living room, watching television. A commercial comes on. It pictures a woman wearing a white uniform and a name badge that reads Mary. She is helping a frail elderly man in a nursing home. The announcer simply says, "Mary cannot afford dental care for her six-year-old child." The commercial cuts to a man toiling over a car in a gas station. The announcer: "Bill will not be able to afford heat for his home this coming winter." In another cut, a woman is seen entering data into a computer. The announcer: "Jane's children are with the neighbors again. She can't afford decent day care." Finally, the commercial cuts to a listless man, dressed in work clothes, sitting in the company cafeteria, surrounded by other workers. The announcer says, "Bill is worried. The car broke down, and there's no money to fix it. He hitched a ride today and was late. He doesn't know what to do tomorrow." The commercial shifts to a screen made up of a mosaic composed of these people. The announcer says, "What do all of these people have in common? They all work full-time. None of them is on welfare. But it is impossible for any of them to make ends meet on their wages, or even to buy the basic necessities of life. None of them sees much hope for the future. And their future is our future. Isn't it time we did something to bring back the American dream?"

In a second television commercial we see a young couple in a dilapidated car, clearly in need of maintenance. They are driving slowly through a pleasant neighborhood, staring at a modest house. The young woman is holding a child. They are looking at the house like children staring at a toy store window. The announcer says, "Over the last fifteen years, the wages of workers in the average young family with children actually dropped by about 15 percent. The house the Bells are looking at will never be theirs. As hard as they work, they can barely hang on to their own apartment. The American dream of owning a home is no longer within their reach. It's time to restore the dream for them."

These are not the commercials we saw in the presidential campaigns of the 1980s. Yet each would have been as accurate then as it would be now. Each could have been packaged no less dramatically than any of the commercials that were shown. Why, then, have we not seen such commercials in electoral campaigns?

The messages contained in these commercials can exert a significant impact on the voting public because they dramatize the very underpinnings of our nation. The American dream is not one in which there is constant suffering and hopelessness on the streets of our nation. Most Americans support assistance to those in distress because they believe that there is a fundamental moral and political obligation to provide economic opportunities to all Americans. For example, public support for solutions to the problem of children living in hunger and inadequate housing grows as we encounter more information about the extent of poverty among the young in our society. We are deeply moved and often shaken by the ironies that underscore the problems: while we root for the people of Hungary and East Germany as they shed the shackles of communism, we discover that there are more Americans living in poverty than there are people in those two countries. We spend four times more money on the Strategic Defense Initiative—a program with little likelihood of success—than on the successful early-education programs of Head Start, at a time when "half the little children who enter our urban primary schools next fall will fail to finish school."[1]

The American ethos is so basic to our society that as citizens we cringe when these urban kids fail on a massive scale. Most Americans intuitively appreciate the importance of opportunity and know that societal assistance to achieve it is "the right thing to do." And when government and politics fail to do the right thing, to fulfill basic obligations, there is growing disenchantment and a sense of loss that is hard to measure in concrete terms but that nevertheless exists. David Broder notes, "Everywhere I went last autumn, I heard rumblings that the Washington insiders had forgotten who put them in power." He echoes those sentiments by noting that the restiveness is in good part due to the fact that "Congress could find money for savings-and-loan bailouts and other 'special interest' needs but not for down-home concerns of average voters."[2] To argue for the worth of public programs that help re-create the American ethos is to appeal to our basic sense of what we are as a nation.

Nevertheless, there is a widely held perception that the public opposes an expansion of governmental action on the domestic social front. Much was written on the public's skepticism, during the Reagan era, toward expanded federal governmental involvement designed to address domestic problems.[3] In the election of 1980, Reagan won with a platform to reduce federal involvement on the domestic social and economic front, and he remained highly popular throughout much of his presidency as he continued to champion this cause.

The view that the public opposes governmental activism with regard to domestic problems is wrong. Major polls have found consistent—indeed, overwhelming—popular support for domestic social programs before, during, and after the 1980 elections.[4] Even in 1984, despite his landslide victory, only 6 percent of the voters indicated that they had voted for President Reagan because of his conservative philosophy.[5] Exit polls taken on the eve of the 1984 elections also showed 80 percent of the voters expressing support for continued or increased levels of federal social expenditures.[6] In fact, public support for social programs, as measured by a *New York Times* / CBS News poll, actually increased between 1980 and 1984.[7] No wonder researchers have pointed to a "substantial ideological gap" between the social policies of the Reagan administration and the views not only of the American public in general but even of "the average Republican who was considerably left of the party's presidential nominee."[8]

Nor is there any indication that the public's interest in supporting broad domestic social programs abated with the election of President Bush. The patterns of the Reagan period appear in even stronger form during the Bush administration. Within a year of the 1988 elections, issues related to poverty, hunger, and homelessness ranked second in the minds of the public, behind drugs, as the most important problems facing the nation. Surveys found that over 60 percent of all Americans wanted to spend more money on a variety of social and health programs and to see sharp reductions in defense spending.[9] In March of 1991, 81 percent of the American public felt that the government was not making enough progress on poverty issues.[10]

Even on the more vividly symbolic issue of "bigger government," the public's position has shifted. The Harris polls indicate that through the last decade there has been a persistent growth of national sentiment for a more active government at the federal level. Despite President Bush's push for his "thousand points of light" outside of the governmental sector, majorities ranging from 73 to 92 percent of the American public say that they want more governmental activity to deal with environmental, homeless, and housing issues. Louis Harris indicates that, compared with the beginning of the decade, "now there are nearly two times as many people who want a more activist government."[11]

The proposal we outlined in chapter 8 will not be entirely antithetical to the views of even many citizens who see government from a strongly conservative perspective. A leading conservative think tank, the Heritage Foundation, has itself advocated expanding the Earned Income Tax Credit program as a way of providing assistance to those who work hard and yet still need help. The Heritage Foundation has been highly critical of the liberal programs of the sixties, holding that many of the programs "empowered bureaucrats, not people." On the other hand, the EITC program aligns with new conservative thinking, the Heritage Foundation officials argue, because its assistance is aimed directly at empowering hardworking Americans who struggle at the margins of the economy.[12]

In a third commercial, a small-business woman sits in her shop, a puzzled look on her face, watching her customers. Sitting by the cash register, she sees one, then another, and then a third look at her merchandise, stare at the price tags, and leave the shop without buying anything. As the action unfolds, the announcer explains, "Mrs. Young's business will go bankrupt this year. Unlike the savings-and-loan institutions, she will not be bailed out by the federal government. She's wondering what went wrong. She doesn't know that in addition to those who are unemployed, there are millions of others who work full-time and are paid wages so low that they cannot make ends meet. They can't afford to shop in her store. Her business and her city's economy suffer from the problem of chronic low wages. When people around us cannot get decent-paying jobs, the entire economy is hurt. When millions are shut out of the American dream, sooner or later it will hurt all of us. Isn't it time to do something about it?"

It is only natural that the costs of calls for increased governmental involvement would also be the subject of concern and possible objection. The proposal outlined in chapter 8 would require around $20 billion a year. This price comes at a time when there is increased competition at the federal level for scarce resources. From the late 1970s through the mid-1980s, the federal government shifted its spending priorities away from domestic programs and toward defense spending. The budget deficit skyrocketed during these years and, in turn, added significantly to the yearly expenditure required to finance the total federal debt. This expenditure for debt financing, coupled with demands both to reduce the budget deficit and to shore up a variety of domestic programs, has resulted in intense competition for the federal dollar. Unforeseen problems, such as the savings-and-loan crisis and costs of the Persian Gulf war, have further fueled that competition.

To a great extent, the fiscal demands of our new program would be offset by the likely growth of the economy that would bring new revenues to government, which we have projected to equal nearly $70 billion in real dollars yearly by the turn of the century, even if the economy's growth is slow compared with prior years.[13] Furthermore, defense outlays that crowded out social spending are scheduled for actual reductions and are unlikely to continue to inhibit social spending as they did in the late 1970s and the first half of the 1980s. Thus, fresh resources should be available to the government even if taxes are not raised. Nor is it certain that the public opposes new taxes for purposes it believes worthwhile. The alleviation of poverty is one of the areas that Americans say is worthy enough to warrant some increase in taxes.[14] A program that bases benefits on the work ethic and that gives people greater incentives to work full-time than to take welfare, and that at the same time involves little bureaucracy, is likely to prove all the more attractive to the public.

Of course, a tax increase is unlikely in the coming years, and many other programs will compete for funds that will become available, including still-unknown new ones. However, regardless of present or new needs, enabling full-time working Americans to achieve self-sufficiency ought to be a high political priority. The reasons are many. We are speaking of an area that says much about the value the nation truly attaches to the work ethic. Indifference is very costly. Americans who vote (or who have given up the privilege) don't sit in bars or churches discussing the morality of the

American ethos, but they do cringe at the thought of millions of children and working parents who go to bed hungry at night, or of the many others who lack basic medical care. The loss of America's "greatness" may temporarily have been recaptured for the public by victory in the Persian Gulf, but the stark realities of hard work without its reciprocating rewards will not disappear in the aftermath of Desert Storm.

The political priority ought to be high, too, because large numbers of citizens would directly benefit. As chapter 8 observed, a program that enables fully employed families to attain self-sufficiency could assist up to twenty-five million Americans who now fall beneath self-sufficiency, with additional assistance given in the form of tax reductions to people moderately above self-sufficiency. In the number of individuals helped, the proposal could rival the largest federal programs such as Social Security or Medicare, but at a small fraction of the cost. The secondary effects of the program would help even more people and add to the political payoffs. Consider, for example, that the program would bring $50 million annually to a city of about half a million people. The beneficiaries will spend much of this $50 million for local products and services, which will enhance the viability of hundreds of small local businesses dependent on the purchasing power of their community's residents. The spin-off and multiplier effects would spread throughout the local economy, to the benefit of thousands beyond the recipients themselves.

A fourth commercial starts with grainy black-and-white film of Henry Ford, walking around a turn-of-the-century Ford assembly line, mugging to the camera, chatting with workers. The announcer says, "Henry Ford understood the nature of free enterprise. That is why he introduced the two-day weekend and paid his employees good wages. He knew that unless he did, they couldn't buy the cars they built." The scene shifts to color, and the inside of a textile manufacturing facility, with people hard at work. The announcer says, "Today, America is in trouble because too many of our workers can't afford to buy the very goods they manufacture. Millions of our workers can't afford even the basic necessities for themselves and their families." The scene shifts again, to the interior of a sparkling new-car showroom. The room is filled with shiny new Fords, one bored sales-man sitting by his desk, and very few customers who are browsing. The announcer continues as the camera focuses in on the face of the bored salesman, "Low wages harm millions of families and do serious damage to our economy. We need to remember what Henry Ford understood so well and come to grips with how little many of our workers earn and how low wages affect the economic advancement of every one of us. When we do, all Americans will be better off. Every one of us."

At a time of rising racial tensions,[15] some may claim that the proposed program would help primarily racial minori-ties. Problems of low-wage employment, welfare, poverty, and homelessness are often perceived to be issues that affect mainly minority Americans. Some politicians have used the current popular suspicion of affirmative action programs to denounce quotas for minorities and the unfair disadvantage at which these "quotas" place whites.[16]

The program proposed in chapter 8 rises above these issues. It would help all fully employed low-wage workers, the largest grouping of whom are male and white. Whichever party chose to support this program could overcome the charge of pit-ting white against black workers, or Hispanics against blacks[17] or Anglos, by giving each of these groups an oppor-tunity to achieve incomes that allow for self-sufficiency. Democrats could advocate this program and not fear the issue of "quotas." They could emphasize action to alleviate the "economic disadvantage of all Americans," one that extended to all groups rather than exclusively on the basis of race.[18] In espousing the program, Republicans could deflect charges of being opposed to equal opportunity without repudiating the conservatives within their party who are opposed to affirmative action programs and to larger fed-eral bureaucracies. Republicans would gain political benefit, especially at a time when they have become increasingly identified with programs—such as cuts in the capital-gains tax—to assist the wealthy at the perceived expense of other Americans.[19] In fact, the beneficiaries of the program—whites, blacks, Hispanics—could be united in a common political cause by either of the two parties under the banner of economic self-sufficiency for all fully employed workers.

In another commercial, two workers are shown on a split screen. Owens, a black male, is working hard in a warehouse. Ackroyd, a white male, is shown bathed in sweat in the midst of a landscaping job. The split screen continues to focus on both as they go about their work. Occasionally they glance over their shoulders at each other. The announcer says in the background, "The problem isn't quotas. The problem isn't affirmative action. Don't let politicians pit Jim Ackroyd against Fred Owens. The problem is that these two Americans, both high school graduates, found the best-paying jobs they could. The problem is that they will work very hard today and that when they get home, they will struggle just as hard to feed their families and to pay their bills. And they won't make it. And they and their children, like millions more across the country, will go to bed hungry tonight. Isn't it time to redirect the great resources of our nation to giving both Mr. Owens and Mr. Ackroyd, and their families, a better shot at the American dream?"

Far from being an electoral liability, a strategy that emphasizes a coherent program to address the income, health care, and educational needs of low-income working Americans could realize significant electoral gains. One such gain might come from the likelihood that a number of nonvoters would return to the polls and vote for candidates willing to take up the issue of self-sufficiency.[20] The problem of nonvoting has reached epidemic proportions in America. In the last presidential election, the turnout fell to a sixty-four-year low of 50.2 percent, and people in the top 20 percent income bracket were almost twice as likely to vote as those in the lowest 20 percent.[21] Research has shown that a major reason for nonvoting is that people feel that their issues are not being represented by candidates for office. A significant view of nonvoters in 1980, for example, was the perceived failure of the candidates to address the issue of jobs and a good standard of living for working Americans. The political scientist John Zipp's research found that a primary reason for nonvoting in 1980 was that when "individuals do not have their interests represented in the political sphere . . . [nonvoting becomes] a chosen form of political action."[22] The emphasis of the campaigns since 1980 does not appear to have done much better.

Would there have been a difference in the outcome of the 1988 elections had the campaigns emphasized different issues? Suppose that the Dukakis campaign had stressed a far-reaching, comprehensive program to assist Americans in economic distress, a program focusing on the rewards that hard work *should* bring to Americans. Would this change in political strategy have altered the outcome of the 1988 elections?

To help answer these questions, we looked to the General Social Survey of 1989, which provides information on a sample of 1,537 citizens. The voting outcome of the survey sample—52.4 percent for Bush and 47.6 percent for Dukakis—was within about 1 percent of the actual outcome of the election. We calculated the potential effects of this electoral strategy on both nonvoters and voters. In this analysis, we took into account the income levels of voters and nonvoters, their attitudes toward assistance to the poor, and a range of cross-pressures that affect their choices of candidates and their decision whether or not to vote.

The conclusion is startling. The potential of a campaign focusing on the economic health of families is substantial. About 65 percent of those who voted felt that the government was doing too little for the poor. In fact, nearly one-quarter (23 percent) of the votes cast for George Bush came from people who lived in *lower-income* households, many of which would directly benefit from programs to assist low-income workers, *and* who also believed that the government was doing too little to help the poor. If merely one in five of them had voted for Dukakis instead of Bush, and even if voters from higher-income families had gone in the other direction, it would have added 2 percent of the total vote to the Dukakis column. Moreover, nearly half (44 percent) of *all* nonvoters both lived in low-income households and believed that the government was doing too little for the poor. Suppose that a mere one-fifth of these low-income nonvoters had decided to vote, aroused by an effective campaign that stressed the concerns of low-income working families. An additional 2.7 percent of the total vote would then have entered the Dukakis column over and above the votes of high-income persons aroused to turn out for the other side. This analysis, set forth in greater detail in the appendix to this chapter, reveals that a forceful presentation of a program to assist low-income workers, rather than being an electoral liability, could have added a net of nearly 5 percent to the Dukakis vote and resulted in a victory for Dukakis by approximately the same margin as that of Bush's actual victory in 1988.[23]

In some ways, we have possibly *underestimated* the potential effect of such a campaign. The General Social Survey asked about respondents' feelings concerning governmental assistance to the poor, not to the *working* poor. It is plausible that a program accenting assistance to the working poor would garner even greater voter support than one designed to help poor citizens regardless of whether they work or not.

Moreover, the analysis does not take into account the many higher-income voters who, for reasons other than direct benefits to themselves, feel that government assistance to the poor has been insufficient. An additional 29 percent of the nonvoters fall into this category. Some of them might find a powerful appeal in this campaign. Our proposal addresses the plight of low-income Americans who work full-time all year long, people who practice self-help and try to fend for themselves. It would also create more educational opportunities for them and open more decent-paying-job opportunities for those not fully employed at present. Such a proposal might well draw strong support from some higher-income Americans who believe that too little is now being done for the poor, especially from among those higher-income voters who made the decision not to vote. Bringing just one in ten of these nonvoters to the polls would add up to another 1.3 million voters, or 1.5 percent of the total.

Of course, we cannot know the actual impact that an emphasis on economic distress would have had on the presidential election of 1988. Numerous variables affect electoral fortunes, and we cannot control for many of them here. Nevertheless, the point this analysis raises is important: a look at the issue preferences and economic circumstances of voters and nonvoters suggests that a campaign stressing self-sufficiency solutions to economic distress could have resulted in a significant political advantage. Only if mishandled could it have been an electoral liability.

Other political advantages of a self-sufficiency initiative are also apparent. An initiative of this type can serve to create and build a foundation that justifies and gives coherence to other programs offering to help Americans reach a better life. Democrats and Republicans alike recognize the hardships that average American families experience today in buying their own house and affording a college education for their children. Numerous members of Congress from both parties are today pressing for a variety of plans that would ease the financial hardships facing American families.[24] Such initiatives to help average families would make more sense when combined with ones to assist fully employed Americans who are now unable to afford even more-minimal basic necessities. Other vital goals of the nation, such as reducing crime and drug abuse, are tied to a program that enables working Americans to achieve self-sufficiency. Most experts would argue, for example, that we can make only modest headway with the problem of crime as long as the alternatives to illegal income remain inadequate earnings or welfare.

The potential electoral advantages do not necessarily end here. A national campaign focusing on issues of economic self-sufficiency could affect other political races as well. For example, of the thirty-three Senate races in the 1988 national election, seven were decided by less than 5 percent of the vote,[25] with four victories going to the Republican side and three to the Democratic side. Had the pattern described for the presidential election been repeated in these races, four Republican senators elected by a close margin might have lost. Conversely, had the Republicans made economic self-sufficiency an issue, the presidential race itself might have turned into a virtual landslide, and the Republican party could have picked up an additional three Senate seats.

These results would not have been trivial. The addition of four Democratic senators would have given the party sixty in all, and thus a significantly better chance of overriding the many presidential vetoes and winning other votes on the floor that Democrats now lose by narrow margins. A majority of this size would also have guaranteed Democratic control of the Senate through the 1992 elections. Likewise, the alternative of additional victories for the Republicans would have left the Democrats with a razor-thin majority in the Senate, ensuring that vetoes would have been sustained and that many more floor votes would have gone to the Republicans, and would have left the minority party poised in subsequent elections to take control of the Senate, needing only two seats to do so.

The reanalysis of the 1988 election can lead to no firm conclusions. No one can know exactly what would have happened had one or both of the campaigns been different in emphasis and style, let alone what might happen in future elections. However, this reexamination does provide information about the potential that exists for a candidate or party that champions the cause of securing self-sufficiency for all fully employed Americans. The potential is to enlarge one's vote significantly and to turn the tide in closely contested elections.

In another commercial, a large flag flies in the foreground, while in the background victorious American troops are embracing next to a charred battleground somewhere in the Iraqi desert. The announcer intones, "The war is over. We won. As Americans, we are rightfully proud of what we have achieved. American bravery, intelligence, and hard work were successful." The scene gradually shifts to a factory where American workers produce U.S. flags. Men and women, blacks, whites, Asians, and Hispanics are all working side by side. The announcer continues, "These are also brave Americans. They work hard, too. But here, at home, we haven't won the war yet. The workers who make the flags we fly, the homes we live in, and the clothes we wear don't have wages that give them a chance at the American dream." The camera focuses in on one of the workers, with sweat beading on his face. As it does, the announcer says, "Bill makes $11,000 a year. His income does not provide the essentials to take care of his family. It's time for all Americans to have real opportunity. It's time to win the war at home."

Since the potential for electoral success that we have described is a projection, not confirmed truth, it will still require political leadership that is both strong and willing to take risks in order to bring the issue of low-wage employment to center stage in an election campaign. Many insightful observers of American politics believe that such political leadership is lacking on the domestic front. David Broder says that politicians today are preoccupied by "trivial pursuits" on domestic issues: by "such topics as flagburning, dirty records and government funding of offensive art."[26]

Robert Kuttner writes that whereas a generation ago we were creating programs to address the plight of the middle and lower classes, today we are kept busy avoiding the true economic issues by focusing on capital gains tax cuts rather than on realistic remedies to economic problems.[27] An even more pessimistic assessment comes from the analysis of public opinion polls. For example, in studies of the public's response to homelessness, the *Washington Post* / ABC News, the *New York Times* / CBS, and the Harris polls found that despite the belief that "the government can do a lot about homelessness" and despite the willingness of 65 percent of the public to pay more in taxes to help the homeless, 80 percent of all Americans doubted that they would see an end to the problem in their lifetimes. Why is there such pessimism? The polls reveal a broad sense of compassion, but very little confidence among most Americans that anything will really change. The pollsters attribute this situation to the absence of passionate political leadership on this and other social issues.[28] Yet, as we argued in chapter 8, there *are* solutions that could significantly change the world of both the fully employed and the marginally employed who now live in economic distress.

But even if political leadership with the requisite passion and commitment fails to materialize in presidential election campaigns, action is still possible. Important social legislation can gain congressional approval even if it has not been at the center of election campaigns. Recently, legislation on such critical issues as day care, civil rights, and even an enlargement of the Earned Income Tax Credit program has passed both houses of Congress without having first become a pivotal item on the national electoral agenda. In a similar manner, a program to bring self-sufficiency to fully employed Americans can become a salient element of Congress's public policy agenda as long as members of Congress do not feel that the issue will harm their chances of getting reelected. The proposal we recommend would appear to be politically feasible. It is consistent with public opinion, addresses the views of mainstream liberals and conservatives alike, rewards the work ethic and creates incentives for getting a job, avoids pitting minorities and women against one other or against white males, creates no new bureaucracies, and does not require an increase in taxes. Members of Congress can enact legislation without fearing an electoral backlash; in fact, they can use the legislation as a method of unifying disparate parts of their political constituencies.

In the decade of the nineties, it is to be hoped, elected officials will champion public policies that resolve the issues of economic self-sufficiency and limited educational possibilities that today confront millions of our citizens. The nation needs a passionate recommitment to the idea that all hardworking Americans can make their way. Only then can America be true to its ideals.

What would have happened if the Dukakis campaign had emphasized a far-reaching, comprehensive program to assist Americans in economic distress, while highlighting the work ethic and the rewards that work should bring? The non-voters who would have been most likely to vote because they favored or opposed such a campaign would have been primarily those who felt that the government was doing too little or too much to help the poor. Even then, we could project an added turnout of no more than one-fifth of these potential voters. If these nonvoters' participation had risen by one-fifth, total participation would have grown from 50 percent to about 58 percent of all eligible voters. Such a turnout is not unreasonable; it is a level slightly beneath actual voter participation in the 1960s.[29]

Still other considerations would have affected the turnout and voting of nonvoters.[30] For one, cross-pressured non-voters would have been far less likely to decide to turn out than the nonvoters who found no such conflicts. The cross-pressured would have been people who would have supported Dukakis but felt that government was giving too much assistance to the poor, and people who would have supported Bush but felt that government was giving too little assistance to the poor. Another consideration would have involved income. Higher-income nonvoters would have been more likely to cast votes than lower-income nonvoters. Table 23 shows the relationship between attitudes toward governmental assistance to the poor and household income among nonvoters.

Using these assumptions, we calculated[31] the potential vote of the 1988 nonvoters and added that figure to the total of those who did vote in the election. The mobilization of the nonvoters on each side, given the aforementioned assumptions, added to the actual vote would have given Dukakis a

T a b l e 2 3
DISTRIBUTION OF NONVOTERS IN THE 1988 ELECTIONS, BY FAMILY
INCOME AND ATTITUDES TOWARD GOVERNMENT ASSISTANCE TO THE
POOR (N = 225, IN FREQUENCIES)

| Family Income | Attitudes toward Government Assistance | |
	Too Little	Right or Too Much
Up to $25,000	99	34
Over $25,000	65	27
Percentage of Nonvoters	72.9	27.1

Source: General Social Survey, NORC.

slim lead over Bush, 50.2 percent to 49.8 percent.

It is plausible, too, that a campaign emphasizing con-
certed action to help low-income working Americans would
have influenced the direction of the vote of those who actually
voted in the 1988 elections. Consider, for example, those
with higher incomes who voted for Dukakis but thought
that too much governmental assistance was going to the poor.
Surely, some of them would have turned away from Dukakis
on the basis of their dislike for a campaign whose center-
piece was a program that would have given even more assistance to low-income Americans. Suppose that 20 percent of
these voters had voted for Bush. Similarly, suppose that 20
percent of those with lower incomes who voted for Bush but

T a b l e 2 4
THE DISTRIBUTION OF VOTES IN THE 1988 PRESIDENTIAL ELECTION, BY FAMILY
INCOME AND ATTITUDES TOWARD GOVERNMENT ASSISTANCE TO THE POOR
(N = 407, IN FREQUENCIES)

| Votes Cast for | Family Income below $25,000 | | Family Income above $25,000 | |
	Too Little	Right or Too Much	Too Little	Right or Too Much
Dukakis	83	12	72	27
Bush	48	27	64	74
Percentage for Dukakis	63.4	30.8	52.9	26.7

Source: General Social Survey, NORC.

Table 25
ALTERNATIVE OUTCOMES FOR THE PRESIDENTIAL ELECTION OF
1988 (IN PERCENTAGES OF THE VOTE)

	Percentage of Votes Cast for:	
	Dukakis	Bush
Votes Cast as Reported in GSS Survey	47.6	52.4
Outcome with 20% Turnout for Nonvoters with Intensity of Preference	50.3	49.7
Outcome with 20% Non-voter Turnout Added along with Shifts among Actual Voters	52.3	47.7

Source: General Social Survey, NORC.

who believed that too little governmental assistance was going to the poor had decided to vote for Dukakis on the basis of their support for a program that would have assisted low-income families, a program that could well have directly benefited many of them. Table 24 shows the relationship between attitudes toward governmental spending, household income, and candidate choice among the voters. The possible shift among these voters would have added 2 percent to the Dukakis vote, giving Dukakis 52.3 percent of the vote and Bush 47.7 percent (see table 25).

APPENDIX

Further Economic Considerations about the Proposed Program

A number of economic objections may be leveled against the program we propose, beyond those discussed in chapter 8, and we address these here. One likely question is whether the program will end up affecting the work effort of recipients. Consider the program's tax rate on every additional dollar earned (the marginal tax rate). Table 26 shows that when a family of four moves from an income of, say, $16,000 to one of $22,000, its total after-tax income would rise from $18,655 to $21,815, an increase of $3,160. An increase in gross income of $6,000 would thus result in an after-tax increase that is $3,160, or about 47.5 percent less (the marginal tax rate is therefore 47.5 percent).

Some analysts may believe this to be a marginal tax rate so high as to reduce the incentive for such workers to be employed or, if employed, to work hard. It is to be noted that this rate is considerably less than the present one of greater than 60 percent on low-income working Americans, as EITC, food stamp, and rent supplement benefits decrease

Table 26

AFTER-TAX INCOMES TO FAMILIES OF FOUR EARNING INCOMES OF $16,000 AND $22,000 UNDER THE PROPOSED PROGRAM (IN DOLLARS)

Family Income	Tax Credit	Total Income before Tax	Tax	Total Income after Tax
16,000	4,275	20,275	1,620	18,655
22,000	2,775	24,775	2,960	21,815

with rising earnings, coupled with the federal and Social Security taxes on those earnings. In any case, the marginal rate is unlikely to reduce the incentive to be employed—*indeed to have at least one worker employed full-time and a second worker employed at least half-time,* or the equivalent of this—because the supplements, which raise most workers' earnings by significant amounts, require this level of employment for eligibility. Nor is the marginal tax likely to diminish the workers' incentive to work hard on the job in order to earn raises. For families at income levels below the line of self-sufficiency, every extra dollar of take-home earnings reduces the chief problem most of these families face. This is the problem of being able to pay utility bills without cutting into the already slim food budget, or being able to pay for automobile insurance without cutting into the housing budget. For these fully employed workers, the incentive to earn more take-home pay is very high. As we saw in chapter 8, a large number of families even with incomes as much as one-third above the threshold of self-sufficiency report that they have difficulty affording food, clothing, medical care, and housing. As a result, the incentive to get wage raises is also high for fully employed workers in many of the families with incomes somewhat above the line of self-sufficiency, let alone at or beneath that line. In any case, the marginal tax rate suggested here is not an essential element of the proposal. It would be possible to lower it with no dilution of the concept or objective of the program, although to do so would lead to a higher cost to the government.

An allied objection is that supplements given to low-wage employment will simply be used by employers to reduce the wages they offer. If so, the effect of the program will simply subsidize the employer and partly or mostly counteract the supplements to the workers. This is sometimes known as the Speenhamland effect, after the experiment begun during the late eighteenth century in Speenhamland, Berkshire, England, to supplement the earnings of poor agricultural workers. The Speenhamland system operated quite similarly to both the EITC and the proposed supplement program in that governmental funds were used to increase wages considered too low to enable workers to afford necessities. It is said that the Speenhamland system led to a depression of wages and to the unproductive use of labor in Speenhamland and elsewhere where the scheme was introduced. The Report of the Royal Commission to Investigate the Poor Laws so concluded in 1834,[1] as did policymakers and social scientists for many years thereafter.[2] However, a recent investigation that used modern social science methods to reanalyze the data available to the royal commission, and that also analyzed additional information, has found otherwise. Mounting evidence suggests that the wage subsidies of the Speenhamland system had virtually no effect either on the level of wages employers offered or on the productive use of labor.[3] No such negative effect has been demonstrated, either, with respect to the present Earned Income Tax Credit.

Nor is it likely that an expanded supplement program will be much different. Employers ordinarily will have no idea which of their employees receives supplements, or how much they receive, because employers will not have access to information upon which the supplements are based. Whether employees receive supplements or not, and how much they receive, will depend both on whether their spouses are employed at least half-time and on how much total income the family has, including the earnings of the second spouse. This information will generally be unavailable to employers unless both spouses happen to work in the same establishment. In addition, because the absolute amount of the supplement depends on these factors as well as on the size of the household, workers will not all be alike. Some will receive no supplement, and those who do will receive supplements in varying amounts. In fact, it will be difficult for employers to set wage rates as a function of the supplements even if they know the approximate amount of the supplements coming to their employees, and they ordinarily will not. To do so, they will have to set different wage rates for individual employees rather than according to job classifications, since the supplements that workers in the same job and wage level receive will vary considerably in size.

A completely different kind of economic objection concerns the proposed program's effect on family stability. If the program were to enable a parent to become financially better-off after separation from a spouse, it might encourage family separations. Recall, however, that the proposal applies only to fully employed individuals and their families. If a separated parent were to retain the children, that parent would have to be employed full-time the entire year in order to become eligible for the supplements. As a result, the program represents an option almost diametrically opposed to the one usually associated with welfare today, in which single parents normally receive welfare benefits only if they are not fully employed. The proposed program would give an adult a financial incentive to separate from his or her spouse only if that adult were prepared to be fully employed and his or her spouse had been unwilling to do so.

NOTES

1 THE AMERICAN ETHOS AND THE AMERICAN PEOPLE

1. The findings of the book focus on 1989, the seventh and final year of the longest continuous recovery during peacetime in the nation's history. Since this recovery ended late in the summer of 1990, the book also contains findings up through the spring of 1990. To determine whether the year 1989 was an aberrant recovery year, we examined the two years prior to it, obtaining results for each of the years similar to those for 1989. In addition, the book presents research going back to the early 1960s, reviewed in chapter 5, so as to be able to detect long-term developments.

2. Adam Smith, *The Wealth of Nations* (London: Methuen, 1930), p. 80.

3. Louis Hartz, *The Liberal Tradition in America: An Interpretation of American Political Thought since the Revolution* (New York: Harcourt, Brace, and World, 1955), p. 207.

4. Quoted in Robert N. Bellah et al., *Habits of the Heart: Individualism and Commitment in American Life* (New York: Harper and Row, 1985), p. 33.

5. Franklin was by no means alone at the start of the Republic in his belief that America was unique among nations as a place where all industrious persons could advance. There were many others, some cited in the newspapers even today. For example, a letter published in the *New York Times* in October 1990 quoted these words of Charles Pinckney, South Carolina representative at the Constitutional Convention: "There are fewer distinctions . . . of rank than of any other nation," Pinckney said, and "hence arises a greater equality than is

to be found among people of any other country, and an equality which is most likely to continue, because in a new country, possessing immense tracts of uncultivated land, there will be few poor, and few dependent." Andrew G. Celli, Jr., letter to the editor, *New York Times,* October 26, 1990, p. A34. Thomas Jefferson held a similar view. He wrote that there would not be poverty in America, comparable to that in Europe, "as long as there are vacant lands for [workers] to resort to; because whenever it shall be attempted by the other classes to reduce them to the minimum of subsistence, they will quit their trades and go to laboring the earth." Quoted in John F. Manley, "American Liberalism and the Democratic Dream," *Policy Studies Review,* 10 (Fall 1990): 96. The spirit of the time was described by Alexis de Tocqueville half a century later in his famed *Democracy in America:* "In America then everybody finds facilities, unknown elsewhere, for making or increasing his fortune."

6. Bellah, *Habits of the Heart,* p. 33.

7. Gary Scharnhorst, *Horatio Alger, Jr.* (Boston: Twayne, 1980), p. 69.

8. Horatio Alger, Jr., *Struggling Upward and Other Stories* (New York: Crown, 1945), pp. 203 and 205.

9. Nowhere did the stirring ideal that freedom could bring about advancement of the individual and the inclusion of all who were industrious in the good life find more powerful expression than in Adam Smith's *Wealth of Nations.* Published in 1776, this book eventually gained a popularity in America unsurpassed anywhere else. Smith wrote that individual freedom coupled with the division of labor, which he called the "progressive economy," would produce increasing wealth and a rising demand for labor. In such an economy, Smith argued, higher wages would become commonplace and be extended to the "lowest ranks of people." He believed that wherever individuals were free and willing to take the initiative and work hard not only would the lower ranks do better but the dynamic of the progressive economy ultimately would have an equalizing effect:

> The whole of the advantages and disadvantages of the different employments of labour and stock must, in the same neighbourhood, be either perfectly equal or continually tending to equality. If in the same neighbourhood, there was any employment evidently either more or less advantageous than the rest, so many people would crowd into it in the one case, and so many would desert it in the other, that its advantages would soon return to the level of other employments. This at least would be the case in a society where things were left to follow their natural course, where there was perfect liberty, and where every man was perfectly free . . . to chuse what occupation he thought proper. . . . (*The Wealth of Nations,* p. 101)

10. Cited in Irvin G. Wyllie, *The Self-Made Man in America: The Myth of Rags to Riches* (New Brunswick: Rutgers University Press, 1954), pp. 201–4.

11. Quoted in Michael B. Katz, *In the Shadow of the Poorhouse: A Social History of Welfare in America* (New York: Basic Books, 1986), p. 7.

12. Quoted in Michael Lewis, *The Culture of Inequality* (New York: New American Library, 1978), p. 7. Other characteristics Sumner ascribed to the poor were idleness and extravagance.

13. For a historical survey of the often contemptuous attitudes toward the poor in

America, see Katz, *In the Shadow of the Poorhouse*. The law professor Kenneth Karst nicely stated the American view that sees the dependent poor as lesser citizens when he observed, "To be a citizen is to be a member of a moral community, to be a responsible person, not a ward of society." See Kenneth L. Karst, *Belonging to America: Equal Citizenship and the Constitution* (New Haven: Yale University Press, 1989), p. 141. Ronald Reagan made a similar point in his first inaugural address, in 1981, when he asked whether the nation should not provide opportunity to the poor "to make them self-sufficient so they will be equal in fact and not just in theory." See *Ronald Reagan: Public Papers of the President of the United States* (Washington, D.C.: Government Printing Office, 1982), p. 2. For more-detailed discussions, see Lee Rainwater, *What Money Buys: Inequality and the Social Meanings of Income* (New York: Basic Books, 1974), and Michael Walzer, *Spheres of Justice: A Defense of Pluralism and Equality* (New York: Basic Books, 1983), esp. pp. 105–8.

14. See Nicholas Lemann, *The Promised Land: The Great Black Migration and How It Changed America* (New York: Alfred A. Knopf, 1991), pp. 149–51, and James T. Patterson, *America's Struggle against Poverty, 1900–1985* (Cambridge: Harvard University Press, 1986), pp. 135–36.

15. U.S. Bureau of the Census, *Statistical Abstract of the United States, 1982–83* (Washington, D.C.: Government Printing Office, 1982), p. 340, table 554; p. 376, table 625, and p. 440, table 727.

16. Critiques of the War on Poverty are found in Charles Murray, *Losing Ground: American Social Policy, 1950–1980* (New York: Basic Books, 1984); Lawrence M. Mead, *Beyond Entitlement: The Social Obligations of Citizenship* (New York: Free Press, 1986); and Allen J. Matusow, *The Unraveling of America: A History of Liberalism in the 1960s* (New York: Harper and Row, 1984). Defenses of the War on Poverty are contained in Theodore K. Marmor et al., *America's Misunderstood Welfare State: Persistent Myths, Enduring Realities* (New York: Basic Books, 1990); Sheldon H. Danziger, Robert H. Haveman, and Robert D. Plotnick, "Antipoverty Policy: Effects on the Poor and Nonpoor," in Sheldon H. Danziger and Daniel H. Weinberg, eds., *Fighting Poverty: What Works and What Doesn't* (Cambridge: Harvard University Press, 1986), pp. 50–77; and John E. Schwarz, *America's Hidden Success: A Reassessment of Twenty Years of Public Policy* (New York: W. W. Norton, 1983).

17. George Gallup, *The Gallup Poll: Public Opinion 1989* (Washington, D.C.: Scholarly Resources, 1990), p. 184.

18. *Weekly Compilation of Presidential Documents* 24, no. 1 (1988): 241.

19. Lawrence Mead, *The New Politics of Poverty* (New York: Basic Books, 1992), p. 6.

20. This development of opinion about the poor is described and documented in ibid.

21. Calculated from James R. Kleugel and Eliot R. Smith, *Beliefs about Inequality: Americans' Views about What Is and What Ought to Be* (New York: Aldine de Gruyter, 1986), p. 58, table 3.8, column entitled "Very Important Cause."

22. Ibid.

23. Ibid., p. 79, table 4.2.

24. Gallup, *Gallup Poll*, p. 183.

25. Speaking for the nation's governors, the chairman of the National Governors' Association, Bill Clinton, said in 1987 that the welfare system must "provide genuine opportunity for people to reach maximum self-sufficiency that we all agree should be at the heart of our welfare system." U.S. House of Representatives, Committee on Education and Labor, *Family Welfare Reform Act of 1987: Report together with Minority and Additional Views*, pt. 2, 100th Cong., 1st sess., August 7, 1987, p. 21. Views of members of the two parties in the House are found in the same source.

26. Republicans focused on the generous, in their view, benefits that welfare offered, coupled with the paucity of work requirements. See U.S. House of Representatives, Ways and Means Committee, *Family Welfare Reform Act of 1987: Report together with Additional and Dissenting Views*, pt. 1, 100th Cong., 1st sess., June 17, 1987, pp. 175–77.

27. In committee reports during the debate on welfare reform, the Democratic majority said that the reforms it proposed were "designed . . . to promote self-support through work" and devoted to "helping [welfare] families become self-supporting." See ibid., p. 37. The Republican minority agreed that this was the reform's purpose. The Republicans wanted a reform, they said, that would "provide to welfare recipients the opportunity to gain education and employment training in order to become self-sufficient and productive in our society." See House Committee on Education and Labor, *Family Welfare Reform Act of 1987*, p. 100.

28. Even the staunchest advocates of public assistance programs have held this view. In the words of Franklin Roosevelt, "Continued dependence upon relief induces a spiritual and moral disintegration fundamentally destructive to the national fiber. . . . We must preserve not only the bodies of the unemployed from destitution but also their self-respect, their self-reliance and courage and determination." Quoted in Fred Block et al., *The Mean Season: The Attack on the Welfare State* (New York: Pantheon Books, 1987), p. 31.

29. The importance of the exploitation of natural resources to the development of American industrial power is demonstrated in Gavin Wright, "The Origins of American Industrial Success, 1879–1940," *American Economic Review* 80 (September 1990): 651–68.

3 ECONOMIC SELF-SUFFICIENCY IN PRESENT-DAY AMERICA

1. Quoted in William J. Eaton, "The Poverty Line," *New York Post*, April 4, 1970, magazine, p. 4.

2. One standard definition, found in *Webster's New World Dictionary of the American Language, College Edition* (New York: World, 1954), p. 1144, says that poverty is "a deficiency in necessary properties," implying "a lack of the resources for reasonably comfortable living." The dictionary points out that "poverty" has a broader meaning than do terms such as "destitution," which convey a lack of the necessary means for survival or subsistence. If it were true

that "poverty" normally referred to an absence of the means for survival, as does "destitution," the oft-used term "extreme poverty" would have no meaning, just as the term "extreme destitution" does not and is therefore never used.

3. It is clear that Orshansky's use of the term "average family budget" was deliberate and tied to the idea that poverty was relative to the standard of living then prevailing in the nation. She explained her decision to use the average family budget in "How Poverty Is Measured," *Monthly Labor Review,* February 1969, p. 38.

4. Orshansky, herself, asserted that she had defined the poverty threshold in terms "consistent with the standards of living prevailing in this country." See ibid. In its review of the history of the official poverty line, the Department of Health, Education, and Welfare makes this same observation: "The poverty measure used by the Census Bureau . . . is an attempt to specify in dollar terms a minimal level of income adequacy for families of different types, *in keeping with American consumption patterns.*" See U.S. Department of Health, Education, and Welfare, *The Measure of Poverty: Technical Paper II,* September 1, 1976, p. 8 (italics ours). Orshansky made it equally clear elsewhere in her writings that she did not use destitution as the foundation for her measure but instead a standard connected to the level of living prevalent in the United States. See, for example, Mollie Orshansky, "Counting the Poor: Another Look at the Poverty Profile," *Social Security Bulletin,* January 1965, p. 5. In a 1970 interview, Orshansky defined poverty in this manner: "To be poor is to feel deprived of those goods and services and pleasures which others around us take for granted as a right." Quoted in Eaton, "Poverty Line," p. 4.

5. In Orshansky's words, "The threshold is defined as an attempt to specify the minimum money income that could support an *average* family of given composition at the lowest level of living prevailing in this country." See "How Poverty Is Measured," p. 38 (italics ours). Orshansky had stated this view earlier, in 1965, in "Measuring Poverty," *The Social Welfare Forum, 1965* (New York: Columbia University Press, 1965).

6. See note 2.

7. Quoted in Eaton, "Poverty Line."

8. Although officials started to adjust the official poverty line by the rise in the general consumer price index, the relation of the economy food plan to the total poverty-line income remained near one-third as late as 1990. In 1980, the economy food budget (now called the thrifty food budget) was about $2,710 over a year for a family of four, or 32.2 percent of the $8,414 poverty-line income for that year. In 1990, the thrifty food budget for a family of four was $3,960 over a year, which was 29.6 percent of the poverty-line income of $13,360 for that year.

9. According to the expenditure weights contained in the consumer price index calculated closest to 1980—the period 1982–84—food composed 20.4 percent of the average family budget; it had composed 33.5 percent in 1960.

10. The Lamberts' income in the late 1980s, adjusted to 1990 dollars, was slightly above $22,300. However, this $22,300 measures the amount of income needed for a family of four. The Lamberts are a family of five.

11. U.S. Bureau of the Census, *Statistical Abstract of the United States, 1982–83*

(Washington, D.C.: Government Printing Office, 1982), p. 465, table 763. The budgets are called urban budgets, but they cover communities with 2,500 or more people.

12. A voluminous literature raises diverse questions about the official poverty line. See, for example, Patricia Ruggles, *Drawing the Line: Alternative Poverty Measures and Their Implications for Public Policy* (Washington, D.C.: Urban Institute Press, 1990); Timothy M. Smeeding, Michael O. Higgins, and Lee Rainwater, *Poverty, Inequality, and Income Distribution in Comparative Perspective* (New York: Harvester Wheatsheaf, 1990); Susan E. Mayer and Christopher Jencks, "Poverty and the Distribution of Material Hardship," *Journal of Human Resources* 24 (1989): 88–114; Robert Rector et al., "Dispelling the Myth of Income Inequality," *Backgrounder* (Washington, D.C.: Heritage Foundation, June 6, 1989); Mollie Orshansky, "Commentary: The Poverty Measure," *Social Security Bulletin*, October 1988, pp. 22–24; A. B. Atkinson, "On the Measurement of Poverty," *Econometrica* 55 (1987): 749–64; Timothy M. Smeeding, "Approaches to Measuring and Valuing In-Kind Subsidies and the Distribution of Their Benefits," in Marilyn Moon, ed., *Economic Transfers in the United States* (Chicago: University of Chicago Press, 1984), pp. 139–71; Sheldon Danziger and Peter Gottschalk, "The Measurement of Poverty: Implications for Antipoverty Policy," *American Behavioral Scientist* 26 (1983): 739–56; Peter Townsend, *Poverty in the United Kingdom* (Harmondsworth, Eng.: Penguin Books, 1979); A. K. Sen, "Issues in the Measurement of Poverty," *Scandinavian Journal of Economics* (February 1979): 285–307; Martin Rein, "Problems in the Definition and Measurement of Poverty," in Louis A. Ferman et al., eds., *Poverty in America* (Ann Arbor: University of Michigan Press, 1968), pp. 116–33; and Victor R. Fuchs, "Redefining Poverty and Redistributing Income," *Public Interest* 8 (Summer 1967): 88–95.

13. The minimum cost to feed a family of four a nutritionally adequate diet in 1981 was $244.45 a month, or $2,933.40 a year. Nutrition constituted 20.4 percent of the average family budget (see note 9); that is, the average family budget was 4.9 times larger than its food budget. Multiplying the least-cost food budget ($2,933.40) by 4.9 results in a sum of $14,373.66.

14. Another issue regarding the official poverty line also arose. The income included in calculating it was direct cash income that came, for example, from employment, Social Security, unemployment benefits, or welfare. It did not include in-kind subsidies that met particular needs like food stamps, Medicaid, or housing assistance. A number of households living on direct cash income beneath the official poverty line would not have been counted as officially poor if the income they received from the in-kind programs had entered the calculation. This is an important point if the official poverty line properly reflects the amount of income (whether from cash or in-kind assistance) required to purchase basic necessities. On the other hand, the issue largely dissolves if an income significantly above the official poverty line properly reflects the needed income. By the time households reach the Department of Labor's lower budget (166 percent of the official poverty line when last measured) or reach even 150 percent of the official poverty line, for example, they receive only small amounts, if any, of these in-kind benefits. For male-present families with children living at

125 to 150 percent of the official poverty line in 1989, the average amount of in-kind income received in food stamps and housing assistance was $170 a year. For female-headed families with children living at 125 to 150 percent of the official poverty line, the average amount was $312. Calculated from the U.S. House of Representatives, Committee on Ways and Means, *Overview of Entitlement Programs: 1991 Green Book* (Washington, D.C.: Government Printing Office, May 7, 1991), table 59, p. 1043, and table 61, p. 1046.

15. Quoted in Leonard Larsen, "The Odd Ascent of William Bennett," *Arizona Daily Star*, December 31, 1990, p. 12.

16. Glenn Collins, "Robin Leach Seeks Only Comfort, Not Riches," *Arizona Daily Star*, December 6, 1990, p. C1.

17. See table 3 for results from 1981 through 1987. The Gallup survey results are calculated from *Gallup Report*, no. 248 (May 1986): 3, for 1981 through 1986 and from our own tabulation for 1987 on the basis of the tapes of the Gallup poll, January 16–19, 1987. The question was not asked after 1987.

18. A third such poll was carried out in 1989 but did not contain information on household size necessary to determine the relation between household income and the official poverty line.

19. Since respondents to the Gallup poll reported their incomes in broad rather than interval categories and the number of respondents in the survey is comparatively small (1,500) as compared with the Current Population Survey, the income categories we use with the Gallup poll are broader (100 to 150 percent of the official poverty line) than those of the Current Population Survey (100 to 125 percent and 125 to 150 percent of the poverty line). Although if one uses the Gallup poll the number of cases drops below fifty, a majority of the respondents (52.7 percent in 1984; 54.6 percent in 1987) whose income is between 125 and 150 percent of the poverty line in the Gallup poll report that they cannot afford at least one of the necessities throughout the year.

20. Chapter 2 described 1988 as a typical year for the Lambert family. During 1988, its income totaled $22,300. That year the official poverty line for a family of five was $14,305; the Lamberts' income was thus 156 percent of the official poverty line. For the Bartelles, a family of four, 1989 was a typical year, in which their income was about $18,500. The official poverty line for a family of four in 1989 was $12,675, so the Bartelles' income was 146 percent of the official poverty line.

21. Calculated from the tapes of the Gallup poll, January 16–19, 1987, on the basis of the median response.

22. Based on an analysis of the tapes of the Gallup poll, January 1987. Of the respondents in rural areas, 55.7 percent with incomes of 100 to 150 percent of the poverty line said that they could not afford one or more of the necessities at some time during the year; of those with similar incomes from suburban areas, 53.4 percent said the same; and of those from urban areas, 64.5 percent did. The percentages of respondents with incomes from 150 to 200 percent of the poverty line who could not afford one or more of the necessities were as follows: rural residence, 31.4 percent; suburban residence, 35.9 percent; urban residence, 36.9 percent. Also, when the Department of Labor last formulated its family budgets, it calculated budgets for families in metropolitan and in

nonmetropolitan areas, finding that the lower family budget was only about 5 percent greater in the former than in the latter. See Bureau of the Census, *Statistical Abstract of the United States, 1982–83,* p. 465, table 763. Although the costs for food, housing, and medical care were higher in metropolitan areas, the Department of Labor found that they were largely offset by higher transportation costs in the nonmetropolitan areas (p. 465, table 763). On the other hand, when the Gallup poll asked respondents about the smallest amount of money a family needs to live in their communities, the median answer of those in urban and suburban areas came to 184 percent of the official poverty line but the answer of those in rural communities came to 139 percent of that line. The evidence regarding costs by locational differences is thus mixed at present. A final answer as to whether distinctions by urban-suburban-rural location ought to be made must come from an examination of data that are substantially more extensive and detailed than those currently available. The Congress has requested such a study. The evidence we have at present does not warrant making urban-rural distinctions.

23. Spencer Rich, "Food Stamps Found to Fall Short: Poor Pay More for Staples in Underserved Areas, Two Studies Show," *Washington Post,* May 18, 1990, p. A17.

24. For persons living in heavily populated central cities, the housing costs on the economy budget would be inadequate, perhaps by as much as $2,000 a year, but would be largely offset by the ability of such persons to depend on reliable mass transportation rather than having to purchase private transportation.

25. See Christopher Jencks and Kathryn Edin, "The Real Welfare Problem," *American Prospect,* Spring 1990, p. 35.

26. See pp. 47–48, below, for evidence.

27. See pp. 47–48, below, for evidence.

28. A study carried out in three sites (Seattle, Yakima, and Pend Oreille) in the state of Washington found that 26 percent of all families containing a full-time worker whose income was beneath 185 percent of the official poverty line were hungry. See Governor's Task Force on Hunger, *Hunger in Washington State,* October 1988, appendix, pp. 4–6, tables 2.S, 2.Y, and 2.PO. Children from families experiencing hunger, in all three sites, were more likely to suffer from fatigue and inability to concentrate and from health problems (pp. 18, 25, 32). A survey covering seven states estimated that more than five million American children under the age of twelve are hungry; it found that hungry children are more than four times more likely to suffer from fatigue than nonhungry children; more than twelve times as likely to report dizziness; almost three times as likely to suffer from concentration problems; and twice as likely to have frequent headaches, ear infections, and colds. See Community Childhood Hunger Identification Project, *A Survey of Childhood Hunger in the United States* (Washington, D.C.: Food Research and Action Center, 1991), p. 11.

29. Michael de Courcy Hinds, "Uninsured Drivers Create Other Kinds of Wreckage," *New York Times,* September 3, 1990, p. 10. The figure is for 1988.

30. Based on an analysis of the tapes of the Current Population Survey, March 1990. About 19 percent of all households beneath 150 percent of the official poverty line—almost one in five—have no telephone.

31. For a family of five, the economy budget in 1988 allows up to $580 a month for the cost of housing, utilities, and telephone. The Lamberts in 1988 spent about $620, or $40 a month more, totaling $480 over the year.

32. Evidence suggests that to obtain housing, people with incomes beneath even the official poverty line may have to spend the amount contained in the economy budget. A staff study of the Joint Economic Committee of Congress in 1989 found that households beneath the official poverty line in 1985, on the average, spent 56 percent of their income on housing (calculated from the study's findings on the assumption that half the poor own their homes and half rent them). A family of four that in 1990 spent 56 percent of its income on housing, and that did spend $6,200 on housing as allowed in the economy budget, would have an income of about $11,100, or $2,260 beneath the $13,360 that marked the official poverty line. See "Alternative Measures of Poverty" (Staff Study Prepared for the Joint Economic Committee, October 18, 1989), table 2.

33. See Michael E. Stone, *One-third of a Nation: A New Look at Housing Affordability in America* (Washington, D.C.: Economic Policy Institute, 1990), pp. 7 and 9, tables 2 and 4.

34. Katherine Swartz, *The Medically Uninsured: Special Focus on Workers* (Washington, D.C.: Urban Institute, July 1989), p. 10, chart 9B.

35. Ibid., p. 4, chart 3B.

36. In a *Washington Post* story in 1990, Diana Seeger of Grand Rapids, Minnesota, who has no medical insurance, was quoted as saying, "If you've never raised a family without medical insurance and don't qualify for Medicaid [because your family income exceeds the Medicaid cutoff], it may be difficult for you to understand the terror parents face when they awake to find a crying baby is running a temperature of 106 degrees." See Victor Cohn, "Rationing Medical Care," *Washington Post National Weekly Edition*, August 13–19, 1990, p. 11. An individual interviewed for this study, Barbara Wellstone, worked full-time but, like Diana Seeger, had no medical insurance. When she became pregnant, she was unable to find prenatal care that she could afford. Her reaction to being turned down for prenatal care because she did not have enough money, she said, resembled that of a woman she had seen on television who faced the same problem. "It made me feel like dirt," she said.

37. Stephen H. Long and Jack Rogers, "The Effects of Being Uninsured on Health Care Service Use: Estimates from the Survey of Income and Program Participation" (Paper delivered at the Annual Meeting of the Allied Social Sciences Associations sponsored by the Society of Government Economists, Atlanta, December 28, 1989), table 3.

38. Reported in Natalie Angier, "Uninsured Are Less Likely to Get Hospital Care, Study Finds," *New York Times*, September 12, 1990, p. A28.

39. Quoted ibid.

40. Quoted in Cohn, "Rationing Medical Care," p. 11.

41. See note 28 above.

42. John E. Chubb and Terry M. Moe, *Politics, Markets, and America's Schools* (Washington, D.C.: Brookings Institution, 1990), p. 108, table 4–5. The number of learning tools in the homes of students distinguished the students from

high-performance schools from those from low-performance schools significantly more than whether there were two parents in the home, whether the
mother was employed, whether either the mother or the father closely moni-
tored the schoolwork of their children, or whether the parents expected their
children to attend college.

43. The total yearly cost of these items for a family of four is about $500.

4 AMERICA'S FAMILIES, AMERICAN WORKERS, AND
ECONOMIC HARDSHIP: THE SCOPE OF THE PROBLEM

1. Calculated from the tapes of the Current Population Survey, March 1990, as
are all figures in this chapter, unless otherwise noted.

2. See chapter 3.

3. More than half the older Americans whom Social Security and Supplemental
Security Income helped raise above the official poverty line were left beneath
the threshold of self-sufficiency.

4. This was no artifact of the approaching recession of late summer 1990. Both
one and two years earlier, the situation had been substantially the same. For
example, in March 1989, 10.2 percent of all full-time workers lived in households with incomes beneath self-sufficiency (calculated from the tapes of the
Current Population Survey, March 1989).

5. If defined as all people who reside in high-poverty urban locales (census tracts
in the 100 largest standard metropolitan areas with poverty rates above 40
percent), the underclass numbered 3.7 million Americans in 1979. See Erol R.
Ricketts and Isabel V. Sawhill, "Defining and Measuring the Underclass," *Journal
of Policy Analysis and Management* 7 (1988): 319, table 1. The authors themselves define the underclass as including considerably fewer people, about 2.5
million (p. 321). The number of American adults and children receiving welfare in 1989 came to 10.9 million.

6. The figures are based on data from the tapes of the occupational section of the
Current Population Survey, March 1990, for machine operators, fabricators
and assemblers, health service workers, farmers and farm operators, building
laborers, freight and material handlers, carpenters, cleaners, personal service
workers, production inspectors and testers, transportation workers, precision
product workers, mechanics, supervisors and proprietors, and protective services workers; from the industry section for furniture workers, repair service
workers, textile and apparel workers, social service workers, and retail workers.

7. David Hoffman, "Bush Seeks to Sew Up Flag Vote," *Washington Post*, September 21, 1988, p. A14.

8. Marianne Yen, "Inside the Factory, Hopes of Prosperity Have Flagged,"
Washington Post, October 16, 1988, p. A3.

9. Ibid.

10. Calculated from the tapes of the General Social Survey, 1983 through 1989.

11. Calculated from the tapes of the General Social Survey, 1989. Of all eligible
voters in 1988 who were employed, 59 percent in households with incomes

of o to 100 percent of the official poverty line were registered to vote; 54 percent with household incomes at 100 to 150 percent of the poverty line; and 84 percent with household incomes above 150 percent of the poverty line. Of all these voters at the three income levels who were registered, the percentages who voted were 65 percent, 82 percent, and 88 percent, respectively. On the relationship between other forms of political activity and income, see Sidney Verba and Norman H. Nie, *Participation in America: Political Democracy and Social Equality* (New York: Harper and Row, 1972), esp. pp. 95–100.

12. *San Antonio Independent School District et al.* v. *Rodriguez et al.,* U.S. Reports, October Term, 1972, 411 US 1, p. 37.

13. Based on calculations from the tapes of the Gallup poll, January 16–19, 1987. Of households at 100 to 150 percent of the official poverty line, 53.4 percent said that they worried all or most of the time about whether they had enough money to pay the bills, compared with 49.6 percent of households below the official poverty line and 22.8 percent of the households with incomes greater than 150 percent of the poverty line.

14. To make this estimate, we set the rate of insufficiency of all workers under the age of 35 at 5.6 percent (the same as the overall rate for fully employed workers above 35); the rate for workers between 35 and 44 at the same 5.6 percent, instead of their actual 6.5 percent; and the rates for workers aged 45–54 and 55–64 at their actual rates of 5.0 percent. This resulted in an overall rate for workers aged 16–64 of about 5.4 percent, or 4.2 million workers.

15. For the rates of formal education in the United States for the adult population at large and for different age groups, see U.S. Bureau of the Census, *Statistical Abstract of the United States, 1990* (Washington, D.C.: Government Printing Office, 1990), p. 134, table 217.

16. Even if every adult American had earned at least a high school degree so that there were no high school dropouts, nearly five million fully employed workers would remain living beneath self-sufficiency. This estimate is based on reducing the rate of insufficiency of all fully employed high school dropouts to 8.4 percent, the same as the rate for workers with a high school degree, and leaving the other rates of insufficiency as they are now.

17. It might be said that some of these fully employed workers who fell beneath self-sufficiency in 1989 perhaps were not so deprived in 1988, or might not be so in 1990. Undoubtedly, some movement both out of and into economic insufficiency exists. Yet the American ethos assumes that people will be able to make their own way regularly if they work long and hard, not merely at times or episodically. Many of these fully employed workers living in poverty have reached their thirties, forties, and fifties, and the nation was in 1989 at the apex of its longest continuous economic recovery ever.

18. The awful choice these millions of families face between poverty and having a parent at home to care for the children comes clear in Barbara Bush's injunction to the graduating students of Wellesley College when she said, "Those human connections with spouses, with children, with friends are the most important investment you will ever make. . . . Fathers and mothers, if you have children, they must come first." *Washington Post,* June 8, 1990, p. C4.

5 WORKING AMERICANS AND ECONOMIC HARDSHIP: THE
COMPLEXITY OF THE PROBLEM

1. Illustrative works on the effect of race and gender on employment and earnings
   are Claudia Dale Goldin, *Understanding the Gender Gap: An Economic History of American Women* (New York: Oxford University Press, 1990); Barbara F. Reskin and Patricia A. Roos, *Job Queues, Gender Queues: Explaining
   Women's Inroads into Male Occupations* (Philadelphia: Temple University Press,
   1990); Reynolds Farley and Walter R. Allen, *The Color Line and the Quality
   of Life in America* (New York: Russell Sage Foundation, 1989), esp. pp. 316–
   61; James P. Smith and Finis R. Welch, "Black Economic Progress after Myrdal," *Journal of Economic Literature* 27 (June 1989): 519–65; William Julius
   Wilson, *The Truly Disadvantaged: The Inner City, the Underclass, and Public
   Policy* (Chicago: University of Chicago Press, 1987); Richard B. Freeman and
   Harry J. Holzer, *The Black Youth Employment Crisis* (Chicago: University of
   Chicago Press, 1986); Suzanne M. Bianchi and Daphne Spain, *American Women
   in Transition* (New York: Russell Sage Foundation, 1986), esp. chap. 6; Paula
   England and George Farkas, *Households, Employment, and Gender* (New York:
   Aldine Press, 1986); Naomi T. Verdugo and Richard R. Verdugo, "Earnings
   Differentials among Mexican American, Black, and White Male Workers, *Social
   Science Quarterly* 65 (June 1984): 417–25; and Finis Welch, "Black-White
   Differences in Returns to Schooling," *American Economic Review* 63 (December 1973): 893–907.
2. To make this estimate, we reduced the insufficiency rates of all minority and
   female workers to the rate for white males, 6.4 percent, as if all fully employed
   workers had this same rate.
3. In fact, were we not only able to eliminate all discrepancies in rates along race
   and gender lines but also to couple this with policies that would get everyone
   successfully through high school, somewhat more than four million fully
   employed workers still would be living beneath self-sufficiency. This would
   leave twice as many fully employed working Americans who live in poverty as
   the present official poverty line indicates.
4. See, for example, June O'Neill, "The Role of Human Capital in Earnings Differences between Black and White Males," *Journal of Economic Perspectives*
   4 (Fall 1990): 25–45; Gordon Berlin and Andrew Sum, *Toward a More Perfect Union: Basic Skills, Poor Families, and Our Economic Future* (New York:
   Ford Foundation, 1988); Eric A. Hanushek, "The Economics of Schooling:
   Production and Efficiency in Public Schools," *Journal of Economic Literature*
   24 (September 1986): 1141–77; Robert B. Reich, *The Next American Frontier*
   (New York: Times Books, 1983); and John C. Hause, "Earnings Profile: Ability and Schooling," *Journal of Political Economy* 80 (May–June 1972): S108–
   S138.
5. Quoted in David S. Broder, "Rising Pessimism about U.S. Prospects," *Seattle
   Times,* July 14, 1991, p. A14.
6. The Armed Forces Qualification Test is described in Berlin and Sum, *Toward
   a More Perfect Union,* pp. 85–88.

7. This level requires a second earner in a three-person household to earn at least one-quarter of the household's income in order for the household to reach self-sufficiency. Earnings of $10,500 were slightly beneath half the median yearly earnings for all fully employed workers in 1986, which was $11,100. As a measure, half the median is frequently used to define low wages and poverty. See Bennett Harrison and Barry Bluestone, *The Great U-turn: Corporate Restructuring and the Polarization of America* (New York: Basic Books, 1988), pp. 121–23, figure 5.3 and appendix, table A-2; and Timothy M. Smeeding et al., *Poverty, Inequality, and Income Distribution in Comparative Perspective* (New York: Harvester Wheatsheaf, 1990), pp. 57–59.

8. The National Longitudinal Survey asks the same respondents each successive year about the amount they work and the amount they earn. The information on employment and earnings used here covers the calendar years 1983–86, enabling us to examine employment and earnings for the same individuals over successive years as well as in individual years.

9. Recall that the focus of attention here is on fully employed workers. Blacks with high educational skills continue to experience higher rates of unemployment and underemployment than equivalent white males, which might well result from differential access to employment opportunities.

10. Calculated from the tapes of the Current Population Survey, 1990.

11. *Arizona Daily Star,* September 25, 1990, p. 10.

12. For examples, see Robert Kuttner, *The End of Laissez-Faire: National Purpose and the Global Economy after the Cold War* (New York: Alfred A. Knopf, 1991); Reich, *Next American Frontier;* Lester C. Thurow, *The Zero-Sum Society: Distribution and the Possibilities of Economic Change* (New York: Basic Books, 1980); Harrison and Bluestone, *Great U-turn;* Lawrence B. Lindsey, *The Growth Experiment: How the New Tax Policy Is Transforming the U.S. Economy* (New York: Basic Books, 1990), esp. chap. 13; and Ralph Landau, "U.S. Economic Growth," *Scientific American,* June 1988, pp. 44–52. For a different view on the competitiveness of American industry, see Charles Schultze, "Industrial Policy: A Dissent," *Brookings Review* 2, no. 1 (Fall 1983): 3–12.

13. See Harrison and Bluestone, *Great U-turn,* appendix, table A-2. Harrison and Bluestone defined a low-wage job as one paying half the median earnings for fully employed workers in 1973 expressed in 1986 dollars ($11,104), which amounts to slightly more than 80 percent of the income a three-person household needed for self-sufficiency in 1986. The study defined low-wage jobs for earlier years by adjusting the 1986 figure for inflation in the intervening years.

14. Ibid. It is true, as Harrison and Bluestone show (table A-2), that the proportion of low-wage jobs dropped during the years 1963–73, from 21.4 percent to 13.1 percent. Note, however, that the proportion of American workers in manufacturing industries declined during that period, too, from 30.0 percent to 26.2 percent.

15. We examine here the period until 1988 rather than 1989 because 1988 was the latest year for which data were available enabling us to make comparisons with West Germany.

16. The compensation comparisons between the United States and Germany are calculated for each country in the country's own currency, adjusted for infla-

inflation during the period. Compensation includes both pay and benefits.

17. U.S. Department of Labor, *Handbook of Labor Statistics, 1989* (Washington, D.C.: Government Printing Office, 1989), p. 572, table 149. Based on the average daily exchange rate for the year, the hourly compensations of American and West German manufacturing workers in 1975 were $6.36 and $6.35, respectively; and in 1979, $9.02 and $11.29, respectively, including pay and benefits.

18. See Bart van Ark, "Comparative Levels of Labour Productivity in Postwar Europe" (CEPR Workshop on European Productivity in the Twentieth Century, London, March 1990). Van Ark finds that absolute productivity (gross value added per hour worked in manufacturing) for 1984 was indexed at 226 in the United States, at 148 in West Germany, and at 100 in the United Kingdom. Other advanced countries also lagged behind the United States with regard to the productivity of the entire labor force, as is shown in William J. Baumol et al., *Productivity and American Leadership: The Long View* (Cambridge, Mass.: MIT Press, 1989), p. 92. American observers are becoming increasingly aware of the substantial productivity and cost advantages American industry may have now compared with industries abroad. See the conclusions of Peter Hooper, a Federal Reserve Board economist, reported in Evelyn Richards, "Competitiveness Update: The Tide May Be Turning," *Washington Post National Weekly Edition,* May 27–June 2, 1991, p. 20; Richard McKenzie, *The Decline of America: Myth or Fate?* (St. Louis: Center for the Study of American Business, 1988); and Schultze, "Industrial Policy."

19. American manufacturing competitiveness in world markets may have suffered because the dollar was allowed to become abnormally strong during the early and middle 1980s. For example, the price of the dollar rose from 2.25 German marks in 1981 to 2.55 marks in 1983 and to 2.94 marks in 1985. Compensation costs of the manufacturing workers in the two countries, however, would have reached parity in 1985 at about 2.15 marks to the dollar, which is approximately what the dollar's price had been in 1981.

    With the price of the dollar high, American goods became expensive in international markets, and foreign goods became inexpensive in ours. During this period, our manufacturing foreign trade balance fell by $113 billion, from a positive $12 billion in 1981 to a negative $101 billion in 1985.

    Exchange rates, of course, are partly a product of governmental policies to deal with problems of inflation or unemployment in the national economy. They are not entirely within the control of the government, either. Foreign governments may and often do attempt to manipulate them for purposes of their own national economic strategies.

20. Other possible explanations include the abnormally crowded labor market that built up in the United States from the entry of the baby boom generation from 1964 to 1980, for example, and the declining power of trade unions.

21. Council of Economic Advisers, *Economic Report of the President, 1991* (Washington, D.C.: Government Printing Office, 1991), p. 297, table B-9 and p. 322, table B-32.

22. Ibid., p. 338, table B-46.

23. Ibid.

24. Ibid., p. 344, table C-44. Average real weekly wages have declined by 16 percent.

    Some would say that this very large gap between productivity and wage growth is explained by the slow rise in the overall productivity that occurred during those years in the United States compared with that in other countries. The comparison of the nation's manufacturing sector to Germany's, described on pages 86–87, disputes this conclusion. Although they attained productivity increases somewhat higher than those of West German workers, American manufacturing workers nevertheless received about 30 percent lower increases in compensation. As important, even if the nation's comparatively small overall advance in productivity was the decisive factor behind the disparity between the growths of our productivity and of our wages, little agreement exists about what can be done to improve American productivity. Some economists claim that nonresidential fixed investment is the most important ingredient in productivity improvement. This certainly seems logical. Nevertheless, the sharp downturn in the nation's productivity growth following 1973 happened although real nonresidential fixed investment as a proportion of our GNP was generally greater in the period after 1973 than in the 1950s or 1960s. For the figures, see Henry R. Nau, *The Myth of America's Decline: Leading the World Economy into the 1990s* (Oxford: Oxford University Press, 1990), p. 229. Many economists believe that the nation's investment in the past decade or two may have been placed poorly and that productivity depends upon other factors, too, such as the number of workers entering the labor force (which affects the capital/labor ratio), worker training, and the quality of organization of the workplace. For examples, see Baumol et al., *Productivity and American Leadership,* and Robert B. Reich, *The Next American Frontier* (New York: Times Books, 1983). But disagreements about the combination of other factors important to productivity and about the relative significance of those factors are so profound that no dominant explanation exists among economists to account for productivity change. Indeed, some prominent analysts have concluded that the causes of the downturn in the nation's rate of productivity growth after 1973 are mostly unknown (see Edward F. Denison, *Accounting for Slower Economic Growth: The United States in the 1970s* [Washington, D.C.: Brookings Institution, 1979]), with the result that elevating the rate may be no more than modestly subject to manipulation. Economists differ widely even about the proper way to define and measure productivity in the economy, and these definitional differences often greatly influence their conclusions and policy prescriptions regarding productivity growth. See Baumol et al., *Productivity and American Leadership,* pp. 240–50.

25. One other oft-cited factor—the strong educational and job-training systems in other countries and, as a result, more highly skilled labor forces—also seems an unlikely cause of the prevalence of low-paying jobs in the United States. The productivity of the labor force of the United States has been higher, not lower, than that of the other countries (see note 18). In addition, in the United States full-time employment leaves not only uneducated but many well-educated workers beneath self-sufficiency.

6 OTHER CASUALTIES OF THE JOB SHORTAGE

1. Quoted in Michael B. Katz, *In the Shadow of the Poorhouse: A Social History of Welfare in America* (New York: Basic Books, 1986), p. 17.
2. See Charles Murray, *Losing Ground: American Social Policy 1950–1980* (New York: Basic Books, 1984), and Lawrence M. Mead, *Beyond Entitlement: The Social Obligations of Citizenship* (New York: Free Press, 1985).
3. Quoted in Ronnie Dugger, *On Reagan: The Man and His Presidency* (New York: McGraw-Hill, 1983), p. 109. For an opposing view about the effect of welfare on employment, see David T. Ellwood, *Poor Support: Poverty in the American Family* (New York: Basic Books, 1988), and David T. Ellwood and Lawrence H. Summers, "Poverty in America: Is Welfare the Answer or the Problem?" in Sheldon H. Danziger and Daniel H. Weinberg, eds., *Fighting Poverty: What Works and What Doesn't* (Cambridge: Harvard University Press, 1986), pp. 78–105.
4. Lawrence M. Mead, *The New Politics of Poverty: Nonworking Poverty in the U.S.* (New York: Basic Books, 1992), p. 107. His calculation is that jobs were unavailable to half of the workers listed as unemployed.
5. Quoted in Gary Scharnhorst, *Horatio Alger, Jr.* (Boston: Twayne, 1980), p. 125.
6. Ibid., p. 121.
7. Mark S. Littman, "Reasons for Not Working: Poor and Nonpoor Householders," *Monthly Labor Review*, August 1989, pp. 16–21.
8. Calculated from ibid., p. 19, table 4.
9. Ibid.
10. The findings in this paragraph are calculated from the tapes of the Current Population Survey, March 1990. Of all employed workers, the percentage with incomes beneath self-sufficiency who were employed either full-time or part-time for economic reasons was 10.2 percent.
11. Judith M. Gueron and Edward Pauly, *From Welfare to Work, Summary* (New York: Russell Sage Foundation, 1991), pp. 25, 46; Kathryn H. Porter, *Making Jobs Work: What the Research Says about Effective Employment Programs for AFDC Recipients* (Washington, D.C.: Center on Budget and Policy Priorities, 1990), pp. 28–29; Jay Mathews, "Study Says States May Save Money by Requiring Welfare Recipients to Work," *Washington Post*, May 18, 1990, p. A4; Robinson G. Hollister, Jr., *New Evidence about Effective Training Strategies* (New York: Rockefeller Foundation, 1990), p. 20, table 1 (appendix).
12. Gueron and Pauly, *From Welfare to Work*, p. 46, report that this was strictly enforced in the SWIM program.
13. Gayle Hamilton and Daniel Friedlander, *Final Report on the Saturation Work Initiative Model in San Diego* (New York: Manpower Demonstration Research Corporation, November 1989), p. 12, table 1.
14. Ibid.
15. Hollister, *New Evidence*, pp. 9–10.
16. Ibid., p. 21, table 2 (appendix).
17. Calculated from ibid.

18. John Burghardt and Anne Gordon, *More Jobs and Higher Pay: How an Integrated Program Compares with Traditional Programs* (New York: Rockefeller Foundation, 1990), p. 42, table 2 (appendix).
19. Ibid., p. 12.
20. Ibid., p. 42, table 2.
21. Ibid., p. 12.
22. Hamilton and Friedlander, *Final Report,* p. 5.
23. U.S. House of Representatives, Committee on Ways and Means, *Overview of Entitlement Programs: 1990 Green Book* (Washington, D.C.: Government Printing Office, 1990), p. 618.
24. June O'Neill reaches the same conclusion regarding the impact of the highly publicized ET program in Massachusetts in her study *Work and Welfare in Massachusetts: An Evaluation of the ET Program* (Boston: Pioneer Institute for Public Policy Research, 1990).
25. The information about America Works in this paragraph is from a telephone interview with Peter Coves, its director, in February 1991.
26. The record appears to be similar in the state of Connecticut. Carol J. Castaneda, "The Richest State in the Nation Finds Many in Need of Aid," *USA Today,* July 9, 1991, p. A6, reports that America Works of Connecticut "trained and placed 650 welfare recipients in jobs since 1985." Ellen Graham, "How Private Company Helps Welfare Clients Find and Keep Jobs," *Wall Street Journal,* May 18, 1990, p. 1, puts the figure at somewhat more than 1,000 in those years. The average monthly welfare adult caseload for Connecticut in 1989 alone was more than 35,000.

7 A VIEW FROM CITY HALL

1. For an extensive discussion of this strategy and its practice across the nation, see Peter K. Eisinger, *The Rise of the Entrepreneurial State* (Madison: University of Wisconsin Press, 1988). For a complementary view of the "mixed" strategy approach and its practice in various states, see "Arizona's New Foundations: Economic Development for the 1990's" (Center for Economic Competitiveness, SRI International, Menlo Park, Calif., 1991).
2. Eisinger, *Rise of the Entrepreneurial State,* chap. 5.
3. See "City Fiscal Conditions, 1980–1990: A 50 City Survey" (U.S. Conference of Mayors, Washington, D.C., January 1991). See also Michael Specter, "The New Domestic Tug-of-War," *Washington Post National Weekly Edition,* April 8–14, 1991, p. 6.
4. For a discussion of the "health" of the states, see "States of Austerity", *Washington Post National Weekly Edition,* January 14–20, 1991, p. 34. A *New York Times* survey of twenty major cities showed 75 percent of them toiling under major budget deficits. See "Strapped, Big Cities Take Painful Steps," *New York Times,* January 6, 1991. See also "City Fiscal Conditions."
5. Eisinger, *Rise of the Entrepreneurial State.* For a discussion of the high cost of these programs, see Margery Marzahn Ambrosius, "The Effectiveness of State

Economic Development Policies: A Time-Series Analysis," *Western Political Quarterly* 42 (September 1989): 283–300.

6. See John E. Schwarz and Thomas J. Volgy, "Experiments in Employment—A British Cure," *Harvard Business Review* 66 (March–April 1988): 104–12.

7. See Robert Guskind, "Enterprise Zones: Do They Work?" *Journal of Housing* 47 (January–February 1990): 47–54. See also R. E. Green and M. A. Brintnall, "State Enterprise Zone Programs: Variation in Structure and Coverage" (Center for the Promotion of Policy Relevant Urban Research, University of Wisconsin, Milwaukee, 1986).

8. Guskind, "Enterprise Zones," pp. 52–59. See also Bret C. Birdsong, "Federal Enterprise Zones: A Poverty Program for the 1990's" (Paper given at the Urban Institute, Washington, D.C., October 1990).

9. See "Ranking the Ten Best International Cities," *Bulletin of Municipal Foreign Policy*, Autumn 1990, pp. 45.

10. See Ambrosius, "Effectiveness of State Economic Development Policies," pp. 283–300.

11. See Paul Brace and Gary Mucciaroni, "The American States and the Shifting Locus of Positive Economic Intervention," *Policy Studies Review* 10 (Fall 1990): 163.

12. See Margery Marzahn Ambrosius, "The Role of Occupational Interests in State Economic Development Policy-Making," *Western Political Quarterly* 42 (March 1989): 53–68. Another researcher has looked at the effects of local development policies for 212 cities and found that although there are positive effects on capital investment, these policies have had little impact on employment in those cities. See Richard Feiock, "The Effects of Economic Development Policy on Local Economic Growth," *American Journal of Political Science* 35 (August 1991): 643–55.

13. See "America's Hot Cities," *Newsweek*, February 6, 1989, pp. 42–49; see also "Top 50 Cities," *City and State*, November 19–December 2, 1990, pp. 11–33.

14. Wage rates were calculated on the basis of wages for manufacturing jobs, since the U.S. Department of Labor does not provide statistics on aggregate wage rates for these cities. We contacted Charlotte's economic development officials in an effort to determine which of their strategies had an impact on the working poor. They indicated that they did not know which, if any, of their programs helped generate better-paying jobs. See "Economic Planning and Economic Growth: A Comparison of Tucson to Six Other Cities" (Greater Tucson Economic Council, May 1990).

15. See "Privatization: A Special Report," *Cities Weekly*, November 12, 1990, pp. 1–8. To illustrate the impact of privatization on wages, we can look at two areas of services in Tucson. In one, we privatized special-needs transportation. Although there were some savings for the government, the actual wages of drivers declined by about 40 percent when fringe benefits are included. In a second case, an analysis of privatization of commercial garbage collection showed a 50 percent decline in wages of workers who would shift from the public to the private sector.

16. See "Arizona's New Foundations."

8 THE PATH OF ACTION

1. In 1989, when there were nearly 30 million Americans in working poverty, the Office of Family Assistance of the Social Security Administration recorded that the average monthly number of recipients of AFDC was 10.9 million, including children.

2. Based on median benefits available to a three-person household. Information from the Office of Family Assistance in the Social Security Administration indicates that, in 1989, the median AFDC payment available to three-person households was approximately $390 per month; food stamps available to them would have totaled about $160 a month; families could also receive $290 a month, on the average, in rent supplements or public housing, although only 35 percent on welfare received such assistance. This monthly welfare assistance amounts to $840, or about $10,100 a year. Add $1,500 for Medicaid, and it totals $11,600. A self-sufficiency income for a household of three in 1989 would have been approximately $15,400, and about $14,100 after federal taxes, including the Earned Income Tax Credit adjustment. Consequently, the entire package of welfare was about 82 percent of a self-sufficiency income, after taxes.

3. See note 2.

4. It should be recalled, moreover, that the majority of families on welfare do not receive the entire package described in note 2. For example, while 98 percent and 83 percent received Medicaid and food stamps in early 1990, respectively, only 35 percent received housing assistance. See U.S. House of Representatives, Committee on Ways and Means, *Overview of Entitlement Programs: 1991 Green Book* (Washington, D.C.: Government Printing Office, 1991), p. 1384, table 1.

5. Quoted in U.S. House of Representatives, Committee on Education and Labor, *Family Welfare Reform Act of 1987: Report together with Additional and Dissenting Views,* 100th Cong., 1st sess., August 7, 1987, p. 21.

6. A fully employed worker, as defined here, is employed at least 2,000 hours a year on one or more jobs (this averages out to at least 40 hours a week for at least 50 weeks a year), unless subject to bona fide unemployment because of layoff or as a job loser for no more than six weeks during the year. The unemployment provision could be lengthened for some prescribed period during recessionary periods. Those who were unemployed, though remaining eligible for benefits for the hours they were employed, would not receive benefits other than unemployment compensation for the period they were unemployed.

7. We say "at a minimum," because there are other areas of concern with regard to the living standards of the working poor that are not covered here. A full-scale policy would want to address these areas. Among them are the problems the working poor will have in attaining self-sufficiency when they retire. The self-sufficiency budget contains no room for savings for a pension, except for Social Security. Yet Social Security and other assistance available to the elderly still leave nearly three in ten senior citizens beneath self-sufficiency today. On the need for a poverty-line measure that has a time horizon longer than a single

year, see Harold Watts, "An Economic Definition of Poverty," in Daniel P. Moynihan, ed., *On Understanding Poverty: Perspectives from the Social Sciences* (New York: Basic Books, 1969), pp. 316–29. Nor does the proposal to follow cover even relatively brief absences from work because of sickness or the need to care for ill children. All of our major competitor nations, even Japan, have such programs. These exemplify issues that would have to be addressed in a truly comprehensive policy of worker assurance to bring income security at self-sufficiency levels to the lives of the working poor. In addition, various issues involving employees' needs for recognition, participation, sense of contribution, and power to affect their workplaces merit attention.

8. These are estimates, since the necessary data for 1991 were not available at the time of writing. The incomes for different-size families retain the same ratios that occur in the official poverty line. The self-sufficiency incomes would become a federal standard. Were this standard considered inadequate for some locales, state governments could provide supplements through their own tax systems.

9. For an analogous argument regarding the minimum wage, see Arthur M. Okun, *Equality and Efficiency: The Big Tradeoff* (Washington, D.C.: Brookings Institution, 1975), pp. 20–21.

10. We define dual-adult families as fully employed when the combined employment of the adults equals one and a half full-time workers for a year, or a combined employment of no less than 3,000 hours over the year unless subject to bona fide unemployment (see note 6), or unless the family contains small children (here, one adult who is fully employed would meet the definition). In the cases of households with children headed by single adults, the household is defined as fully employed when the adult is fully employed.

11. House Committee on Ways and Means, *Overview of Entitlement Programs: 1991 Green Book* p. 902.

12. See note 10. This maximum applies to all dual-adult families except those with small children, for which the maximum is a single fully employed worker. Some would argue that a single fully employed worker ought to be the maximum for all families with children, because of the importance of having children, regardless of their ages, cared for by a parent and because the costs of day care and other expenses attendant to employment of a second earner significantly reduce the return of the second earner [see, for example, David T. Ellwood, *Divide and Conquer: Responsible Security for America's Poor* (New York: Ford Foundation, 1987), pp. 19–21]. At the same time, about half of all dual-adult families with children do have second earners in the work force, so the maximum work effort the proposal expects is not excessive in this sense, particularly considering the expectation made for families with small children. This maximum simultaneously leaves room for the adults to decide that one of them will remain home half the time, thereby permitting them greater time and energy for parenting if they feel that year-round full-time employment by both parents precludes or materially undercuts their ability to be effective parents.

13. The after-tax figures here and in the foregoing discussion do not include the EITC, because the program we propose would replace it.

14. For details on how the tax credits would apply to single-adult households with children, see note 15. The present EITC contains a limit on the number of

children that it will support in a household. The credit remains the same for a household with three or more children as for a household with two children. It would be possible, if desired, to place a similar limit on the number of children that our proposed program would support. The new credits, then, would remain the same for households with three or more children as for those with two children. Alternatively, half a credit could be given for a third child.

15. The credits would operate in the same manner for single-adult households with children. For 1991, a family with one adult and two children would need an income of $16,600 to reach self-sufficiency, or $14,600 after taxes (once again, the EITC is excluded from the calculation here, since the proposed program would replace it). A single fully employed worker at the new minimum wage would earn $10,100, or $9,300 after taxes. Income received from the absent parent, as well as all other income, would be added to this. If there were no absent-parent payments or other income, the maximum credit would be $5,300 (the difference between $14,600 and $9,300). As with the present EITC, a limit could be placed on the credit so that it does not enlarge beyond two or three children in a household. The EITC currently contains a limit of two children.

16. See table 2. About 35 percent of the families with incomes of from 150 to 200 percent of the official poverty line nationwide reported that they were unable to afford food, clothing, or medical care at some point during the year. Also, Susan Meyer and Christopher Jencks, "Poverty and the Distribution of Material Hardship," *Journal of Human Resources* 24 (Winter 1989): 88–114, found from a survey in Chicago that 24 percent of the respondents with income from 150 to 249 percent of the poverty line could not afford food throughout the year, and that 32 percent experienced at least two of the ten hardships the authors examined (p. 100, table 3).

17. An analysis of American Housing Surveys shows that more than 40 percent of all four-member households with incomes up to $30,000 in 1987 (or about $34,000 in 1991 dollars) did not have enough money to pay the cost of their shelter after meeting the expenses of nonhousing necessities at a minimum level of adequacy. See Michael A. Stone, *One-third of a Nation: A New Look at Housing Affordability in America* (Washington, D.C.: Economic Policy Institute, 1990), p. 9, table 4.

18. See pp. 146–47.

19. To illustrate, the phaseout of the tax reduction in our proposal could be terminated at, say, an income of $29,000 for a family of four, when the tax reduction would still be about $1,000 per family. This same $1,000 reduction could continue to apply to all families through some still higher income—$50,000 or $60,000—and then phase out after that.

20. Evidence of the relation between wages available to jobholders and crime during the 1980s is cited in Christopher Jencks and Kathryn Edin, "The Real Welfare Problem," *American Prospect,* Spring 1990, p. 34, and Richard B. Freeman and Harry J. Holzer, "The Black Youth Employment Crisis: Summary of Findings," in Richard B. Freeman and Harry J. Holzer, eds., *The Black Youth Employment Crisis* (Chicago: University of Chicago Press, 1986), p. 14.

21. The minimum wage was 54 percent of the average hourly wage in 1950, 52 percent in 1956, 50 percent in 1961, 54 percent in 1968, 46 percent in 1976,

and 45 percent in 1980. See U.S. Bureau of the Census, *Statistical Abstract of the United States, 1982–83* (Washington, D.C.: Government Printing Office, 1982), p. 407, table 677. Setting the minimum wage at $4.85 would be 47 percent of the average hourly wage of $10.38 in June 1991. For the average hourly wage in June 1991, see Council of Economic Advisers, *Economic Indicators,* July 1991, p. 15.

22. Take-up rates have been particularly low for the EITC partly because many low-income workers do not know about the program and do not complete the required tax form. Time and more-vigorous publicity could alleviate this problem.

23. Some of the twelve million workers live in single or dual-adult households with no children and thus would be able to reach self-sufficiency by way of the new minimum wage without tax credits.

24. One adult working full-time for the entire year and the other working half that amount.

25. The supplement could be somewhat higher than this if a family reduced its work level and earnings to take advantage of the education benefit, or if the family contained small children or was headed by a fully employed single parent working at or near the minimum wage (see note 15). The average benefit of $3,000 that we have estimated takes this into account.

26. These households, once more, would need to be fully employed to be eligible.

EPILOGUE: A CALL FOR ACTION; AND APPENDIX
TO THE EPILOGUE

1. Bill Moyers, "America's Vision of the Future" (Keynote Address to the National Legislative Education Foundation, Democratic Issues Conference, March 8, 1991).

2. David Broder, "Back to the Home Front," *Washington Post National Weekly Edition,* March 18–24, 1991, p.4.

3. Vincente Navarro, "The 1984 Election and the New Deal: An Alternative Interpretation," *Social Policy* 15, no. 4 (Spring 1985): 3–10.

4. For an analysis of public opinion polls on this subject, see Vincente Navarro, "Where Is the Popular Mandate? A Reply to Conventional Wisdom," *International Journal of Health Services* 13, no. 3, (1983): 169. See also Everett C. Ladd, "The Reagan Phenomenon and Public Attitudes toward Government," in L. M. Salamon and M. S. Lund, eds., *The Reagan Presidency and the Governing of America* (Washington, D.C.: Urban Institute Press, 1984), 221–49.

5. Navarro, "The 1984 Election and the New Deal," 6.

6. Ibid., 7.

7. R. Pear, "New York Times / CBS News Poll," *New York Times,* December 16, 1984, p. E3.

8. Seymour Martin Lipset, "The Elections, the Economy, and Public Opinion: 1984," *Political Science* 18 (Winter 1985): 28–38.

9. Richard Marin, "A Sea Change on Federal Spending," *Washington Post National Weekly Edition,* August 28–September 3, 1989, p. 37.

10. *Washington Post* / CBS Poll, March 4, 1991.
11. Louis Harris, "A Vote for Activist Government," *New York Times,* November 9, 1989, p. A35; see also Mark Shields, "Why Democrats May Be the Big Winners," *Washington Post,* March 9, 1991, p. A21.
12. See David Broder, "A New Conservative Manifesto," *Washington Post National Weekly Edition,* April 16–22, 1990, p. 4.
13. See pp. 145–46.
14. See Richard Marin, "Marchers for the Homeless Are in Step with the Majority," *Washington Post National Weekly Edition,* October 16–22, 1989, p. 38. A Gallup poll has also found broad public support for tax increases to pay for specific programs, such as helping the homeless and providing long-term health care for the elderly. See Andrew Kohut and Larry Hugick, "Public Supports Higher Taxes for Domestic Programs: Education, Drug War Lead List," *Gallup Report,* no. 289 (October 1989): 4–10.
15. Dale Rogers Marshall, "The Continuing Significance of Race: The Transformation of American Politics," *American Political Science Review* 84 (June 1990): 611–16.
16. See Joel Kotkin and Bill Bradley, "The Democrats and Demographics: The Message Must Change to Meet a New Constituency," *Washington Post National Weekly Edition,* October 19–25, 1990, p. 25.
17. Paula McClain and Albert Karnig, "Black and Hispanic Socioeconomic and Political Competition," *American Political Science Review* 84 (June 1990): 535–45.
18. Stuart E. Eizenstat, "Democrats: We Have Perverted Liberalism," *Washington Post National Weekly Edition,"* September 18–24, 1989, p. 29; see also Robert Kuttner, *The Life of the Party: Democratic Prospects in 1988 and Beyond* (New York: Viking, 1987), pp. 126–27.
19. See Tom Kenworthy, "The Color of Money," *Washington Post National Weekly Edition,* November 6–12, 1989, p. 13; Mark Shields, "Two Cheers for House Democrats," ibid., October 16–22, 1989, p. 30.
20. Robert Kuttner argues for the viability of this strategy, especially for the Democratic party, in his *Life of the Party.* Contrary to the widespread belief that nonvoters, because they are younger, would simply add to the ranks of conservative voters, survey research shows a group of nonvoters who are significantly more flexible in their orientation and potentially favorable to Democratic candidates who advocate issues of economic self-sufficiency. Both the General Social Survey and the University of Michigan's SRC Survey results for the 1988 elections show that nonvoters are younger, poorer, more independent and less Republican, and more moderate or liberal than their voting counterparts.
21. See Paul Taylor, "A National Morale Problem," *Washington Post National Weekly Edition,* May 14–20, 1990, pp. 6–7.
22. John F. Zipp, "Perceived Representation and Voting: An Assessment of the Impact of 'Choices' vs. 'Echoes,' " *American Political Science Review* 79 (March 1985): 50–61.
23. Kuttner, *Life of the Party,* p. 128, comes to a similar conclusion about the potential impact of campaigns directed at attracting Democrats earning $25,000 or less.

24. For example, see William J. Eaton, "Tax Cut Plan Aimed at Middle Class," *Los Angeles Times,* May 7, 1991, A24.

25. The races took place in the following states: Connecticut, which the Democrats won by 49.8 percent to 49.0 percent; Florida, which the Republicans won by 50.4 percent to 49.6 percent; Montana, which the Republicans won by 51.9 percent to 48.1 percent; Nevada, which the Democrats won by 50.2 percent to 46.1 percent; Washington, which the Democrats won by 51.1 percent to 48.9 percent; Wisconsin, which the Democrats won by 52.1 percent to 47.5 percent; and Wyoming, which the Republicans won by 50.4 percent to 49.6 percent. See Richard Scammon and Alice McGillivray, *America Votes: A Handbook of Contemporary American Election Results* (Washington, D.C.: Congressional Quarterly, 1990); and Michael Barone and Grant Ujifusa, *The Almanac of American Politics* (Washington, D.C.: National Journal, 1989).

26. David S. Broder, "Trivial Pursuits," *Washington Post National Weekly Edition,* June 15–July 1, 1990, p. 4.

27. Robert Kuttner, "The Squeeze on Young Families," *Boston Globe,* August 31, 1991.

28. See Richard Marin, "Marchers for the Homeless Are in Step with the Majority," *Washington Post National Weekly Edition,* October 16–22, 1989, p. 38.

29. The General Social Survey, while accurately projecting the outcome of the 1988 elections, understandably underestimates the level of nonvoting. Whereas in 1988 approximately half of all eligible American citizens failed to vote, about one-third in the survey indicated that they did not vote. To correct for this, we treated these nonvoters as if they made up half the sample. Both the General Social Survey and the University of Michigan survey of the 1988 elections show that nonvoters were younger, poorer, more moderate or liberal, and more independent and less Republican than voters.

30. For the characteristics of nonvoters, especially with regard to their party affiliation, political orientation, and income, see the epilogue, n. 20.

31. Working with the figures in table 23, we moved nonvoters to a hypothetical voting distribution for Bush and Dukakis, on the basis of their incomes and attitudes toward governmental assistance to the poor, so that they mirrored the percentages of actual voters in table 24. Next, we revised the table to reflect an increase in the overall turnout of 20 percent, the increased turnout varying with the intensity of the voters' preference (which disproportionately expands turnout) and cross-pressures (which disproportionately lowers turnout). Thus, the least likely to vote would have been those who felt that governmental assistance was "just about right." Most likely to vote would have been those who felt that there was too little assistance to the poor, had family incomes below $25,000, and were likely to vote for Dukakis; or those who felt that there was too much assistance to the poor, had family incomes above $25,000, and were likely to vote for Bush. Closer to the first group in turnout would have been those who were cross-pressured by having attitudes toward governmental assistance opposed by an affinity for the candidate supporting the position different from their own. We then adjusted the results to compensate for income, assuming that higher-income individuals would have been more likely to vote.

APPENDIX: FURTHER ECONOMIC CONSIDERATIONS
ABOUT THE PROPOSED PROGRAM

1. The details of the Poor Law Report of 1834 can be found in Raymond Cowherd, *Political Economists and the English Poor Laws* (Athens: Ohio University Press, 1977), pp. 204–82.
2. See, esp. Karl Polanyi, *The Great Transformation* (New York: Farrar and Rinehart, 1944).
3. See George R. Boyer, *An Economic History of the English Poor Law, 1750– 1850* (Cambridge: Cambridge University Press, 1990), esp. pp. 122–46; Daniel A. Baugh, "The Cost of Poor Relief in South-East England, 1770–1834," *Economic History Review,* 2d ser., 28 (1975): 50–68; Mark Blaug, "The Poor Law Report Reexamined," *Journal of Economic History* 24 (June 1964): 229–45; and idem, "The Myth of the Old Poor Law and the Making of the New," ibid., 23 (June 1963): 151–84.

BIBLIOGRAPHY

Aaron, Henry J. "Alternative Ways to Increase Work Effort under Income Maintenance Systems." In Irene Lurie, ed. *Integrating Income Maintenance Programs*. New York: Academic Press, 1975.
——. "Six Welfare Questions Still Searching for Answers." *Brookings Review* 3
(1984): 12–17.
Abraham, Katherine G. "Structural / Frictional vs. Deficient Demand Unemployment: Some New Evidence." *American Economic Review* 73 (September 1983):
708–24.
Alger, Horatio, Jr. *Struggling Upward and Other Stories*. New York: Crown,
1945.
Ambrosius, Margery Marzahn. "The Role of Occupational Interests in State Eco-
nomic Development Policy-Making." *Western Political Quarterly* 42 (March
1989): 53–68.
——. "The Effectiveness of State Economic Development Policies: A Time-Series
Analysis." *Western Political Quarterly* 42 (September 1989): 283–300.
Anderson, Martin. *Welfare: The Political Economy of Welfare Reform in the United
States*. Stanford, Calif.: Hoover Institution Press, 1978.
Atkinson, A. B. "On the Measurement of Poverty." *Econometrica* 55 (1987): 749–
64.
Auletta, Ken. *The Underclass*. New York: Random House, 1982.
Bane, Mary Jo. "Welfare Reform and Mandatory versus Voluntary Work: Policy
Issue or Management Problem." *Journal of Policy Analysis and Management*
8 (1989): 285–89.

Bane, Mary Jo, and David T. Ellwood. "Slipping into and out of Poverty: The Dynamics of Spells." *Journal of Human Resources* 21 (1986): 1–23.

Banfield, Edward C. *The Unheavenly City Revisited.* Boston: Little, Brown, 1974.

Barone, Michael, and Grant Ujifusa. *The Almanac of American Politics.* Washington, D.C.: National Journal, 1989.

Baugh, Daniel A. "The Cost of Poor Relief in South-East England, 1770–1834." *Economic History Review,* 2d ser., 28 (1975): 50–68.

Baumol, William J., et al. *Productivity and American Leadership: The Long View.* Cambridge, Mass.: MIT Press, 1989.

Bellah, Robert N., et al. *Habits of the Heart: Individualism and Commitment in American Life.* New York: Harper and Row, 1985.

Berlin, Gordon, and Andrew Sum. *Toward a More Perfect Union: Basic Skills, Poor Families, and Our Economic Future.* New York: Ford Foundation, 1988.

Bianchi, Suzanne M., and Daphne Spain. *American Women in Transition.* New York: Russell Sage Foundation, 1986.

Birdsong, Brett C. "Federal Enterprise Zones: A Poverty Program for the 1990's." Paper given at the Urban Institute, Washington, D.C., October 1990.

Blau, Francine D., and Lawrence M. Kahn. "Race and Sex Differences in Quits by Young Workers." *Industrial and Labor Review* 34 (July 1981): 563–77.

Blaug, Mark. "The Myth of the Old Poor Law and the Making of the New." *Journal of Economic History* 23 (June 1963): 151–84.

———. "The Poor Law Report Reexamined." *Journal of Economic History* 24 (June 1964): 229–45

Block, Fred, et al. *The Mean Season.* New York: Pantheon Books, 1987.

Boyer, George R. *An Economic History of the English Poor Law, 1750–1850.* Cambridge: Cambridge University Press, 1990.

Brace, Paul, and Gary Mucciaroni. "The American States and the Shifting Locus of Positive Economic Intervention." *Policy Studies Review* 10 (Fall 1990): 151–72.

Burghardt, John, and Anne Gordon. *More Jobs and Higher Pay: How an Integrated Program Compares with Traditional Programs.* New York: Rockefeller Foundation, 1990.

Burtless, Gary, ed. *A Future of Lousy Jobs: The Changing Structure of U.S. Wages.* Washington, D.C.: Brookings Institution, 1990.

Carson, C. S. "The Underground Economy: An Introduction." *Survey of Current Business* 64, no. 5 (1984): 21–37.

Chubb, John E., and Terry M. Moe. *Politics, Markets, and America's Schools.* Washington, D.C.: Brookings Institution, 1990.

Coleman, James S., et al. *Equality of Educational Opportunity.* Washington, D.C.: U.S. Department of Health, Education, and Welfare, Office of Education, 1966.

Community Childhood Hunger Identification Project. *A Survey of Childhood Hunger in the United States.* Washington, D.C.: Food Research and Action Center, 1991.

Corcoran, Mary, and Greg J. Duncan. "Work History, Labor Force Attachment, and Earnings Differences between the Races and Sexes." *Journal of Human Resources* 14 (1979): 3–20.

Corcoran, Mary, Greg J. Duncan, Gerald Gurin, and Patricia Gurin. "Myth and

Reality: The Causes and Persistence of Poverty." *Journal of Policy Analysis and Management* 4 (1985): 516–36.

Cowherd, Raymond. *Political Economists and the English Poor Laws*. Athens: Ohio University Press, 1977.

Crystal, Graef S. *In Search of Excess: The Overcompensation of American Executives*. New York: W.W. Norton, 1991.

Danziger, Sheldon, Robert Haveman, and Robert Plotnick. "How Income Transfers Affect Work, Savings, and the Income Distribution: A Critical Review." *Journal of Economic Literature* 19 (1981): 975–1028.

———. "Antipoverty Policy: Effects on the Poor and Nonpoor." In Sheldon H. Danziger and Daniel H. Weinberg, eds. *Fighting Poverty: What Works and What Doesn't*. Cambridge: Harvard University Press, 1986.

Danziger, Sheldon, and Peter Gottschalk. "The Measurement of Poverty: Implications for Antipoverty Policy." *American Behavioral Scientist* 26, Number 6 (1983): 739–56.

Denison, Edward F. *Accounting for Slower Economic Growth: The United States in the 1970s*. Washington, D.C.: Brookings Institution, 1979.

Dionne, E. J. *Why Americans Hate Politics*. New York: Simon and Schuster, 1991.

Dugger, Ronnie. *On Reagan: The Man and His Presidency*. New York: McGraw-Hill, 1983.

Dunbar, Leslie. *The Common Interest: How Our Social Policies Don't Work and What We Can Do About Them*. New York: Pantheon Books, 1988.

Duncan, Greg J. *Years of Poverty, Years of Plenty: The Changing Economic Fortunes of America's Workers and Families*. Ann Arbor, Mich.: Survey Research Center, 1984.

Duncan, Greg J., and Saul Hoffman. "On-the-Job Training and Earnings Differentials by Race and Sex." *Review of Economics and Statistics* 61 (November 1979): 594–603.

Duncan, Otis Dudley. "Inheritance of Poverty or Inheritance of Race." In Daniel P. Moynihan, ed. *On Understanding Poverty*. New York: Basic Books, 1968.

Edsall, Thomas Byrne, and Mary D. Edsall. *Chain Reaction: The Impact of Race, Rights, and Taxes on American Politics*. New York: W.W. Norton, 1991.

Eisinger, Peter K. *The Rise of the Entrepreneurial State*. Madison: University of Wisconsin Press, 1988.

Ellwood, David T. *Divide and Conquer: Responsible Security for America's Poor*. New York: Ford Foundation, 1987.

———. *Poor Support: Poverty in the American Family*. New York: Basic Books, 1988.

Ellwood, David T., and Lawrence H. Summers. "Poverty in America: Is Welfare the Answer or the Problem?" In Sheldon H. Danziger and David H. Weinberg, eds. *Fighting Poverty: What Works and What Doesn't*. Cambridge: Harvard University Press, 1986.

Elster, Jon. "Is There (or Should There Be) a Right to Work." In Amy Gutmann, ed. *Democracy and the Welfare State*. Princeton, N.J.: Princeton University Press, 1988.

England, Paula, and George Farkas. *Households, Employment, and Gender*. New York: Aldine Press, 1986.

Farley, Reynolds, and Walter R. Allen. *The Color Line and the Quality of Life in America.* New York: Russell Sage Foundation, 1989.

Feiock, Richard. "The Effects of Economic Development Policy on Local Economic Growth." *American Journal of Political Science* 35 (August 1991): 643–55.

Freeman, Richard B. "Crime and Unemployment." In James Q. Wilson, ed. *Crime and Public Policy.* San Francisco: ICPS Press, 1983.

Freeman, Richard B., and Harry J. Holzer. *The Black Youth Employment Crisis.* Chicago: University of Chicago Press, 1986.

Frey, B. S., and W. W. Pommerehne. "The Hidden Economy: State and Prospects for Measurement." *Review of Income and Wealth* 30 (March 1984): 1–23.

Friedman, Milton. *Capitalism and Freedom.* Chicago: University of Chicago Press, 1962.

Fuchs, Victor R. "Redefining Poverty and Redistributing Income." *Public Interest,* no. 8 (Summer 1967): 88–95.

———. *How We Live: An Economic Perspective on Americans from Birth to Death.* Cambridge: Harvard University Press, 1983.

Galbraith, John K. *The Affluent Society.* Boston: Houghton Mifflin, 1958.

Garfinkel, Irwin, and Robert Haveman. "Income Transfer Policy in the United States." In Edward Seidman, ed. *Handbook of Social Intervention.* Beverly Hills, Calif.: Sage Publications, 1983.

Gilder George. *Wealth and Poverty.* New York: Basic Books, 1980.

Glazer, Nathan. *Affirmative Discrimination: Ethnic Inequality and Public Policy.* New York: Basic Books, 1975.

Goldin, Claudia Dale. *Understanding the Gender Gap: An Economic History of American Women.* New York: Oxford University Press, 1990.

Gordon, David M. *Theories of Poverty and Unemployment.* Lexington, Mass.: Lexington Books, 1972.

Gottschalk, Peter, and Sheldon Danziger. "Macroeconomic Conditions, Income Transfers and the Trend in Poverty." In D. Lee Bawden, ed. *The Social Contract Revisited.* Washington, D.C.: Urban Institute Press, 1984.

Governor's Task Force on Hunger. *Hunger in Washington State.* October 1988.

Green, R. E., and M. A. Brintnall. "State Enterprise Zone Programs: Variation in Structure and Coverage." Center for the Promotion of Policy Relevant Urban Research, University of Wisconsin, Milwaukee, 1986.

Gueron, Judith M., and Edward Pauly. *From Welfare to Work, Summary.* New York: Russell Sage Foundation, 1991.

Guskind, Robert. "Enterprise Zones: Do They Work?" *Journal of Housing* 47 (January–February 1990): 47–54.

Gutmann, Amy, ed. *Democracy and the Welfare State.* Princeton, N.J.: Princeton University Press, 1988.

Hagenaars, Aldi, and Klaas de Vos. "The Definition and Measurement of Poverty." *Journal of Human Resources* 23 (1988): 211–21.

Hamilton, Gayle, and Daniel Friedlander. *Final Report on the Saturation Work Initiative Model in San Diego.* New York: Manpower Demonstration Research Corporation, November 1989.

Hanushek, Eric A. "The Economics of Schooling: Production and Efficiency in Public Schools." *Journal of Economic Literature* 24 (September 1986): 1141–77.

Harrington, Michael. *The Other America: Poverty in the United States.* New York: Macmillan, 1962.

Harrison, Bennett, and Barry Bluestone. *The Great U-turn: Corporate Restructuring and the Polarization of America.* New York: Basic Books, 1988.

Hartz, Louis. *The Liberal Tradition in America: An Interpretation of American Political Thought since the Revolution.* New York: Harcourt, Brace, and World, 1955.

Hause, John C. "Earnings Profile: Ability and Schooling." *Journal of Political Economy* 80 (May–June 1972): S108–S138.

Haveman, Robert H. *Poverty Policy and Poverty Research.* Madison: University of Wisconsin Press, 1987.

———, ed. *A Decade of Federal Antipoverty Programs: Achievements, Failures, and Lessons.* New York: Academic Press, 1977.

Helco, Hugh, and Martin Rein. "Social Science and Negative Income Taxation." In Suzanne Berger, ed. *The Utilisation of the Social Sciences in Policy-Making in the United States.* Paris: Organization for Economic Cooperation and Development, 1980.

Hochschild, Jennifer L. *What's Fair? American Beliefs about Distributive Justice.* Cambridge: Harvard University Press, 1981.

Hollister, Robinson G., Jr. *New Evidence about Effective Training Strategies.* New York: Rockfeller Foundation, 1990.

Jaynes, Gerald David, and Robin M. Williams, Jr., eds. *A Common Destiny: Blacks and American Society.* Washington, D.C.: National Academy Press, 1989.

Jencks, Christopher, et al. *Inequality: A Reassessment of the Effect of Family and Schooling in America.* New York: Basic Books, 1972.

Jencks, Christopher, and Barbara Boyle Torrey. "Beyond Income and Poverty: Trends in Social Welfare among Children and the Elderly Since 1960." In John L. Palmer, Timothy Smeeding, and Barbara Boyle Torrey, eds. *The Vulnerable.* Washington, D.C.: Urban Institute Press, 1988.

Jencks, Christopher, and Kathryn Edin. "The Real Welfare Problem." *American Prospect,* Spring 1990.

Jencks, Christopher, and Paul E. Peterson, eds. *The Urban Underclass.* Washington, D.C.: Brookings Institution, 1991.

Karst, Kenneth L. *Belonging to America: Equal Citizenship and the Constitution.* New Haven: Yale University Press, 1989.

Katz, Michael B. *In the Shadow of the Poorhouse: A Social History of Welfare in America.* New York: Basic Books, 1986.

———. *The Undeserving Poor: From the War on Poverty to the War on Welfare.* New York: Pantheon Books, 1989.

Kaus, Mickey. "The Work Ethic State: The Only Way to Cure the Culture of Poverty." *New Republic,* July 7, 1986, pp. 22–33.

Kleugel, James R., and Eliot R. Smith. *Beliefs about Inequality: Americans' Views about What Is and What Ought to Be.* New York: Aldine de Gruyter, 1986.

Kohut, Andrew, and Larry Hugick. "Public Supports Higher Taxes for Domestic Programs: Education, Drug War Lead the List." *Gallup Report,* no. 289 (October 1989): 4–10.

Kosters, Marvin H., and Murray N. Ross. "A Shrinking Middle Class." *Public Interest,* no. 90 (Winter 1988): 3–27.

Kuttner, Robert. *The Life of the Party: Democratic Prospects in 1988 and Beyond.* New York: Viking, 1987.

———. *The End of Laissez-Faire: National Purpose and the Global Economy after the Cold War.* New York: Alfred A. Knopf, 1991.

Ladd, Everett C. "The Reagan Phenomenon and Public Attitudes toward Government." In L. M. Salamon and M. S. Lund, eds. *The Reagan Presidency and the Governing of America.* Washington, D.C.: Urban Institute Press, 1984.

Landau, Ralph. "U.S. Economic Growth." *Scientific American,* June 1988, pp. 44–52.

Lane, Robert E. *Political Ideology: Why the American Common Man Believes What He Does.* New York: Free Press, 1962.

Lemann, Nicholas. *The Promised Land: The Great Black Migration and How It Changed America.* New York: Alfred A. Knopf, 1991.

Leonard, Paul A., Cushing N. Dolbeare, and Edward B. Lazere. *A Place to Call Home: The Crisis in Housing for the Poor.* Washington, D.C.: Center on Budget and Policy Priorities and Low Income Housing Information Service, April 1989.

Levy, Frank. *Dollars and Dreams: The Changing American Income Distribution.* New York: Russell Sage Foundation / Basic Books, 1987.

Levy, Frank, and Richard C. Michel. *The Economic Future of American Families: Income and Wealth Trends.* Washington, D.C.: Urban Institute Press, 1991.

Lewis, Michael. *The Culture of Inequality.* New York: New American Library, 1978.

Lieberson, Stanley. "A Reconsideration of the Income Differences Found between Migrants and Northern-Born Blacks." *American Journal of Sociology* 83 (January 1978): 940–66.

Liebow, Elliot. *Tally's Corner: A Study of Negro Streetcorner Men.* Boston: Little, Brown, 1967.

Lipset, Seymour Martin. "The Elections, the Economy, and Public Opinion: 1984." *Political Science* 18 (Winter 1985): 28–38.

Littman, Mark S. "Reasons for Not Working: Poor and Nonpoor Households." *Monthly Labor Review,* August 1989, pp. 16–21.

Lynn, Laurence E., Jr. "In Designing Public Welfare Programs, Should Participation in Work and Training Be Voluntary or Mandatory?" *Journal of Policy Analysis and Management* 8 (1989): 284–85.

McClain, Paula, and Albert Karnig. "Black and Hispanic Socioeconomic and Political Competition." *American Political Science Review* 84 (June 1990): 535–45.

McKenzie, Richard. *The Decline of America: Myth or Fate?* St. Louis: Center for the Study of American Business, 1988.

Manley, John F. "American Liberalism and the Democratic Dream." *Policy Studies Review* 10 (Fall 1990): 89–102.

Marmor, Theodore K., et al. *America's Misunderstood Welfare State: Persistent*

Myths, Enduring Realities. New York: Basic Books, 1990.

Matusow, Allen J. *The Unraveling of America: A History of Liberalism in the 1960s.* New York: Harper and Row, 1984.

Mayer, Susan E., and Christopher Jencks. "Poverty and the Distribution of Material Hardship." *Journal of Human Resources* 24 (1989): 88–114.

Mead, Lawrence M. *Beyond Entitlement: The Social Obligations of Citizenship.* New York: Free Press, 1986.

———. "The Hidden Jobs Debate." *Public Interest,* no. 91 (Spring 1988): 40–58.

———. *The New Politics of Poverty.* New York: Basic Books, 1992.

Meyer, Robert H., and David A. Wise. "The Effects of the Minimum Wage on the Employment and Earnings of Youth." *Journal of Labor Economics* 1 (January 1983): 66–100.

Moffitt, Robert A. "The Negative Income Tax: Would It Discourage Work?" *Monthly Labor Review,* April 1981, pp. 23–37.

Moon, J. Donald. "The Moral Basis of the Democratic Welfare State." In Amy Gutmann, ed. *Democracy and the Welfare State.* Princeton, N.J.: Princeton University Press, 1988.

Moon, Marilyn, and E. Smolensky, eds. *Improving Measures of Well-Being.* New York: Academic Press, 1977.

Moynihan, Daniel P. *The Politics of a Guaranteed Income: The Nixon Administration and the Family Assistance Plan.* New York: Random House, 1973.

———. *Family and Nation.* San Diego: Harcourt Brace Jovanovich, 1986.

Moynihan, Daniel P., ed. *On Understanding Poverty: Perspectives from the Social Sciences.* New York: Basic Books, 1969.

Murray, Charles. *Losing Ground: American Social Policy, 1950–1980.* New York: Basic Books, 1984.

National Conference of Catholic Bishops. *Economic Justice for All: Pastoral Letter on Catholic Social Teaching and the U.S. Economy.* Washington, D.C.: Office of Publishing and Promotion Services, 1986.

Nau, Henry R. *The Myth of America's Decline: Leading the World Economy into the 1990s.* Oxford: Oxford University Press, 1990.

Navarro, Vincente. "Where Is the Popular Mandate? A Reply to Conventional Wisdom." *International Journal of Health Services* 13, no. 3 (1983): 152–73.

———. "The 1984 Election and the New Deal: An Alternative Interpretation." *Social Policy* 15, no. 4 (Spring 1985): 3–10.

Novak, Michael, et al. *The New Consensus on Family and Welfare.* Washington, D.C.: American Enterprise Institute, 1987.

Nozick, Robert. *Anarchy, State and Utopia.* New York: Basic Books, 1974.

Okun, Arthur M. *Equality and Efficiency: The Big Tradeoff.* Washington, D.C.: Brookings Institution, 1975.

O'Neill, June. "The Role of Human Capital in Earnings Differences between Black and White Males." *Journal of Economic Perspectives* 4 (Fall 1990): 25–45.

———. *Work and Welfare in Massachusetts: An Evaluation of the ET Program.* Boston: Pioneer Institute for Public Policy Research, 1990.

Orshansky, Mollie. "Counting the Poor: Another Look at the Poverty Profile." *Social Security Bulletin* 28 (January 1965): 3–29.

Orshansky, Mollie. "Measuring Poverty." In *The Social Welfare Forum, 1965.* New York: Columbia University Press, 1965.

———. "How Poverty Is Measured." *Monthly Labor Review,* February 1969, pp. 37–41.

———. "Commentary: The Poverty Measure." *Social Security Bulletin* 51 (October 1988): 22–24.

Palmer, John L., Timothy Smeeding, and Barbara Boyle Torrey, eds. *The Vulnerable.* Washington, D.C.: Urban Institute Press, 1988.

Parker, Hermione. *Instead of the Dole: An Enquiry into Integration of the Tax and Benefit Systems.* London: Routledge, 1989.

Patterson, James T. *America's Struggle against Poverty, 1900–1985.* Cambridge: Harvard University Press, 1986.

Piven, Frances F., and Richard A. Cloward. *Regulating the Poor: The Functions of Public Welfare.* New York: Vintage Books, 1971.

———. *The New Class War: Reagan's Attack on the Welfare State and Its Consequences.* New York: Pantheon Books, 1982.

Plotnick, Robert, and Felicity Skidmore. *Progress against Poverty: A Review of the 1964–1974 Decade.* New York: Academic Press, 1975.

Polanyi, Karl. *The Great Transformation.* New York: Farrar and Rinehart, 1944.

Porter, Kathryn H. *Making Jobs Work: What the Research Says about Effective Employment Programs for AFDC Recipients.* Washington, D.C.: Center on Budget and Policy Priorities, 1990.

Rainwater, Lee. "The Problem of Lower-Class Culture and Poverty-War Strategy." In Daniel P. Moynihan, ed. *On Understanding Poverty.* New York: Basic Books, 1969.

———. *What Money Buys: Inequality and the Social Meanings of Income.* New York: Basic Books, 1974.

Rector, Robert, et al. "Dispelling the Myth of Income Inequality." *Backgrounder* (Washington, D.C.), June 6, 1989.

———. "How Poor Are America's Poor?" *Backgrounder* (Washington, D.C.), September 21, 1990.

Reich, Robert B. *The Next American Frontier.* New York: Times Books, 1983.

Rein, Martin. "Problems in the Definition and Measurement of Poverty." In Louis A. Ferman et al., eds. *Poverty in America.* Ann Arbor: University of Michigan Press, 1968.

Replogle, Ron. *Recovering the Social Contract.* Totowa, N.J.: Rowman and Littlefield, 1989.

Reskin, Barabara F., and Patricia A. Roos. *Job Queues, Gender Queues: Explaining Women's Inroads into Male Occupations.* Philadelphia: Temple University Press, 1990.

Ricketts, Erol R., and Isabel V. Sawhill. "Defining and Measuring the Underclass." *Journal of Policy Analysis and Management.* 7 (1988): 316–25.

Riemer, David Raphael. *The Prisoners of Welfare: Liberating America's Poor from Unemployment and Low Wages.* New York: Praeger, 1988.

Rivlin, Alice. "Helping the Poor." In Alice Rivlin, ed. *Economic Choices: 1984.* Washington, D.C.: Brookings Institution, 1984.

Roback, Jennifer. "Wages, Rents and the Quality of Life." *Journal of Political Economy* 90 (December 1982): 1257–78.

Rowntree, B. S. *Poverty: A Study of Town Life.* London: Macmillan, 1901.

Ruggles, Patricia. *Drawing the Line: Alternative Poverty Measures and Their Implications for Public Policy.* Washington, D.C.: Urban Institute Press, 1990.

Sawhill, Isabel V. "Poverty in the U.S.: Why Is It So Persistent?" *Journal of Economic Literature* 26 (1988): 1073–119.

Scammon, Richard, and Alice McGillivray. *America Votes: A Handbook of Contemporary American Election Results.* Washington, D.C.: Congressional Quarterly, 1990.

Scharnhorst, Gary. *Horatio Alger, Jr.* Boston: Twayne, 1980.

Schultze, Charles. "Industrial Policy: A Dissent." *Brookings Review* 2, no. 1 (Fall 1983): 3–12.

Schwarz, John E. *America's Hidden Success: A Reassessment of Twenty Years of Public Policy* . New York: W. W. Norton, 1983.

Sen, A. K. "Issues in the Measurement of Poverty." *Scandinavian Journal of Economics* (February 1979): 285–307.

Shklar, Judith. *American Citizenship: The Quest for Inclusion.* Cambridge: Harvard University Press, 1991.

Smeeding, Timothy M. "The Antipoverty Effectiveness of In-Kind Transfers." *Journal of Human Resources* 12 (March 1977): 360–78.

———. "Is the Safety Net Still Intact?" In D. Lee Bawden, ed. *The Social Contract Revisited.* Washington, D. C.: Urban Institute Press, 1984.

———. "Approaches to Measuring and Valuing In-Kind Subsidies and the Distribution of Their Benefits." In Marilyn Moon, ed. *Economic Transfers in the United States.* National Bureau of Economic Research, Studies in Income and Wealth, vol. 49. Chicago: University of Chicago Press, 1984.

Smeeding, Timothy M., Michael O. Higgins, and Lee Rainwater. *Poverty, Inequality, and Income Distribution in Comparative Perspective.* New York: Harvester Wheatsheaf, 1990.

Smith, Adam. *Wealth of Nations.* London: Methuen, 1930.

Smith, James P., and Finis R. Welch. "Black Economic Progress after Myrdal." *Journal of Economic Literature* 27 (June 1989): 519–65.

Sowell, Thomas. *Ethnic America: A History.* New York: Basic Books, 1981.

———. *The Economics and Politics of Race.* New York: Morrow, 1983.

Steele, Shelby. *The Content of Our Character.* New York: St. Martin's Press, 1990.

Steuerle, C. Eugene. "Policy Watch: Tax Credits for Low-Income Workers with Children." *Journal of Economic Perspectives* 4 (Summer 1990): 201–13.

Stone, Michael E. *One-third of a Nation: A New Look at Housing Affordability in America.* Washington, D.C.: Economic Policy Institute, 1990.

Sundquist, James L. *Politics and Policy: The Eisenhower, Kennedy, and Johnson Years.* Washington, D.C.: Brookings Institution, 1968.

Swartz, Katherine. *The Medically Uninsured: Special Focus on Workers.* Washington, D.C.: Urban Institute, July 1989.

Taggart, R. *A Fisherman's Guide: An Assessment of Training and Remediation Strategies.* Kalamazoo, Mich.: W. E. Upjohn Institute for Employment Research, 1981.

Tanzi, Vito, ed. *The Underground Economy in the U.S. and Abroad*. Lexington, Mass.: Lexington Books, 1982.

Thon, D. "On Measuring Poverty." *Review of Income and Wealth* 25 (December 1979): 429–40.

Thurow, Lester C. *Poverty and Discrimination*. Washington, D.C.: Brookings Institution, 1969.

———. *The Zero-Sum Society: Distribution and the Possibilities of Economic Change*. New York: Basic Books, 1980.

———. *The Zero-Sum Solution: Building a World-Class American Economy*. New York: Simon and Schuster, 1985.

Townsend, Peter. *Poverty in the United Kingdom*. Harmondsworth, Eng.: Penguin Books, 1979.

U.S. Congress. House. Committee on Education and Labor. *Family Welfare Reform Act of 1987: Report together with Minority and Additional Views*. 100th Cong., 1st sess., August 7, 1987.

U.S. Congress. House. Committee on Ways and Means. *Children in Poverty*. Washington, D.C.: Government Printing Office, 1985.

U.S. Congress. House. Committee on Ways and Means. *Family Welfare Reform Act of 1987: Report together with Additional and Dissenting Views*. 100th Cong., 1st sess., June 17, 1987.

U.S. Congress. House. Committee on Ways and Means. *Overview of Entitlement Programs: Green Book*. Washington, D.C.: Government Printing Office, 1990–91.

U.S. Congress. Joint Committee on the Economic Report. Subcommittee on Low Income Families. *Low Income Families and Economic Stability*. 81st Cong., 1st sess., 1949. Committee Print.

U.S. Department of Health, Education, and Welfare. *The Measure of Poverty: A Report to Congress as Mandated by the Education Amendments of 1974*. Washington, D.C.: Government Printing Office, 1976.

———. *The Measure of Poverty: Technical Paper II*, (Washington, D.C.: HEW, September 1, 1976).

Van Ark, Bart. "Comparative Levels of Labor Productivity in Postwar Europe." CEPR Workshop on European Productivity in the Twentieth Century, London, March 1990.

Van der Gaag, Jacques, and Eugene Smolensky. "True Household Equivalence Scales and Characteristics of the Poor in the United States." *Review of Income and Wealth* 28 (March 1982): 1728.

Van Praag, Bernard M. S., Jan S. Spit, and Huib Van de Stadt. "A Comparison between the Food-Ratio Poverty Line and the Leyden Poverty Line." *Review of Economics and Statistics* 64 (1982): 691–94.

Verba, Sidney, and Norman H. Nie. *Participation in America: Political Democracy and Social Equality*. New York: Harper and Row, 1972.

Verdugo, Naomi T., and Richard R. Verdugo. "Earnings Differentials among Mexican American, Black, and White Male Workers." *Social Science Quarterly* 65 (June 1984): 417–25.

Walzer, Michael. *Spheres of Justice: A Defense of Pluralism and Equality*. New York: Basic Books, 1983.

Watts, Harold W. "Special Panel Suggests Changes in BLS Family Budget Program." *Monthly Labor Review,* December 1980, pp. 3–10.

———. "An Economic Definition of Poverty." In Daniel P. Moynihan, ed. *On Understanding Poverty.* New York: Basic Books, 1983.

———. "Have Our Measures of Poverty Become Poorer?" *Focus* 9, no. 2 (1986): 18–23.

Weisbrod, Burton A., and Lee W. Hansen. "An Income-Net Worth Approach to Measuring Economic Welfare." *American Economic Review* 58 (December 1988): 1315–29.

Welch, Finis. "Black-White Differences in Returns in Schooling." *American Economic Review* 63 (December 1973): 893–907.

Wilson, James Q. *Thinking about Crime.* Rev. ed. New York: Basic Books, 1983.

Wilson, William Julius. *The Declining Significance of Race: Blacks and Changing American Institutions.* Chicago: University of Chicago Press, 1980.

———. *The Truly Disadvantaged: The Inner City, the Underclass, and Public Policy.* Chicago: University of Chicago Press, 1987.

Wright, Erik Olin. "Race, Class, and Income Equality." *American Journal of Sociology* 83 (May 1978): 1368–97.

Wright, Gavin. "The Origins of American Industrial Success, 1879–1940." *American Economic Review* 80 (September 1990): 651–68.

Wyllie, Irvin G. *The Self-Made Man in America: The Myth of Rags to Riches.* New Brunswick: Rutgers University Press, 1954.

Zipp, John F. "Perceived Representation and Voting: An Assessment of the Impact of 'Choices' vs. 'Echoes.' " *American Political Science Review* 79 (March 1985): 50–61.

INDEX

italicized page numbers refer to tables